Wise Wives and Warlocks

Wise Wives and Warlocks

*A rogues' gallery of
East Lothian witchcraft*

compiled by
David McK Robertson

The Grimsay Press

Published by:

The Grimsay Press
An imprint of Zeticula Ltd
The Roan
Kilkerran
KA19 8LS
Scotland
http://www.thegrimsaypress.co.uk

First published in 2013

ISBN 978-1-84530-144-6

Contents

Illustrations

Introduction

East Lothian is well known as the setting for the notorious "North Berwick" witchcraft outbreak, which is so famous as to have come to dominate all consideration of Scottish witchcraft. This is a pity, as there is much about "North Berwick" which is not typical of Scottish witchcraft, while there is a vast amount of other interesting material which up to now has been virtually ignored.

A few years ago I set myself the task of combing the National Archives of Scotland to try to find every reference on record relating to witchcraft and other kindred matters in East Lothian. The results were published in "Goodnight my servants all" (Grimsay Press, 2008). "Wise wives and warlocks" takes a less academic approach, and offers a close look at some of the more interesting characters involved.

Until recently, the politically correct view of Scottish witchcraft was more or less that it was all nonsense, and that "witches" were poor innocent souls unjustly hounded to a horrible death by tyrannical misogynist religious fanatics. While there is a limited amount of truth in this view, we need not doubt for a moment that there were substantial numbers of people in 17th Century Scotland making a living as healers, charmers, and practitioners of traditional magic. Some of these worthies were not above using their "powers" to cause harm and mischief, and some were seriously unpleasant people habitually extracting money and gifts with threats and menaces.

The question of diabolic witchcraft is more problematic. The Devil was originally a foreign import into the world of traditional Scottish magic, and while we cannot absolutely rule out the possibility of "witch clubs" with a "devil" as a sort of master of ceremonies, it seems likely that most of the witchcraft confessions involving the Devil were exercises in telling interrogators what they wanted to hear.

We should perhaps make an effort to climb down from our lofty modern superiority, and try to see magic and witchcraft through 17th Century eyes. Our ancestors were not being wilfully stupid or perverse. Magic and witchcraft were realities which pervaded everyday life, and fitted logically into the scheme of things. Many of our cherished 21st Century notions may seem just as bizarre three hundred years into the future.

David McK Robertson, August 2013.

Agnes Sampson

Not far from the hillfoot village of Humbie in East Lothian stands the imposing mansion house of Keith Marischal. The oldest part is an L-shaped tower house completed around 1589 by George Keith, Earl Marischal of Scotland, possibly incorporating an earlier dwelling. Its construction apparently included a shipload of timber sent by the King of Denmark as a grateful acknowledgement of Keith's good offices in helping to arrange the marriage of the Danish king's daughter Anne to James VI, King of Scots.

A short distance to the north-east, a couple of cottages mark the site of the village of Nether Keith, dwelling place of Agnes Sampson, the "Wise Wife of Keith". The description "matron-like" at the time of her trial for witchcraft in 1591 would suggest someone in middle age, perhaps in her late forties or fifties, indicating a date of birth around the 1540s. Agnes had been married, and had a family – "sons" and "daughters" are mentioned in the records – but by the time Agnes came to the attention of the authorities her husband was dead and at least one of her daughters was married. Agnes may have been married to a man named Brown. Janet Kennedy, the Witch of Redden, recalled receiving a message brought by Agnes's daughter, "a woman named Brown". Since a woman in those days took her surname from her father and retained it after marriage, Agnes Sampson's husband must have been named Brown, if the Witch of Redden's statement is true – something which is far from certain. Agnes earned a living as a midwife and practitioner of traditional magic, which of course explains her familiar by-name "The Wise Wife of Keith".

Nether Keith: Agnes Sampson, the Wise Wife of Keith, lived here. So did Sara Cranstoun, a high-profile associate of the Peaston witches who seems to have been too respectable to prosecute.

Not only skilled in dealing with childbirth and its attendant pains and dangers, as a "Wise Wife" Agnes could cure disease in humans and animals, diagnose and counteract witchcraft, and tell whether a patient would live or die. She was also not averse to causing misfortune for those who deserved it. It is difficult to judge what Agnes held the source and essence of her powers to be. She claimed to have been taught by her father, so she must have regarded her skill at least partly as something which could be learned and acquired. It is also perfectly obvious from her rituals that she believed she could call upon God's power to help her. Then again, she purported to be able to summon a spirit in the form of a black dog named Eloa which would answer questions for her, something which hints at the primeval practices of shamanism. She made occasional use of herbal remedies, and probably also believed that certain actions and forms of words were powerful in themselves. Also, it seems likely that as with modern "magicians", she made liberal use of deception, illusion, and psychology, and would be happy to let the public assume she had occult powers and abilities. The authorities, however, were in no doubt about the origins of Agnes's powers. In the eyes of the Kirk and the Law she derived all her power from the Devil.

Whatever the origins of her power, Agnes had a formidable reputation across East and Midlothian, and beyond, and travelled widely in the practice of her profession. She was sent for, not only by the poor and ignorant, but by the gentry who were supposed to know better.

Since Agnes was a midwife, it is not surprising that she should take steps to reduce her patients' labour pains. Thus we find her giving Effie McCalzean, an Edinburgh lady, a stone bored through with a hole, to be laid under her pillow, and graveyard earth rolled up in a piece of paper with dried and powdered human tissue, to be hidden in her hair. When her labour pains began, Effie's husband's shirt was to be immediately taken off him, folded, and laid under the foot of her bed. The records assure us that during the birth of

Effie's first son her pains were successfully taken off her and laid upon a dog. A cat was the unfortunate recipient of the pains during the birth of another son, and both animals were reported to have run off, never to be seen again.

Agnes could apparently diagnose illness by probing the patient's body with her fingers, and by the smell of a sick person's linen. Sometimes the patient's shirt alone would be sent to her, without the patient. She cured the Lady Kilbaberton with iris root steeped in wine, but her usual method of healing was by "prayer and incantation".

When Agnes was consulted about a seriously ill patient, she would first recite a prayer, sometimes in the patient's presence, sometimes before visiting. If the recitation "stopped" once – that is, presumably, if she faltered or stumbled once in the recitation, this meant that the patient was bewitched. If she stumbled twice, it meant that the patient would die. Now, since Agnes had a reputation to keep up, there would be no point in her wasting her attention on hopeless cases, so if she was summoned to someone who was obviously at death's door, no doubt she would make very sure that she stumbled twice. Here is her prayer, described in the legal records as her "devlish prayer":

> I trow in Almychtie God that wrocht
> baith heavin an erth and all of nocht.
> In his dear son Chryst Jesu,
> in to that anaplie lord I trow,
> wes gotten of the Haly Ghaist,
> borne of the Virgin Marie,
> stoppit to heaven that all weill thane
> and sittis at his faderis rycht hand;
> He bade us cum and ther to dome
> baith quick and deid as he thocht conuene.
> I trow als in the Haly Ghaist,
> in Haly Kirk my hoip is maist,
> that halyschip qhuar hallowars winnis

to ask forgivenis of my sinnis,
and syne to ryis in flesh and bane
the lyff that never mair be gane.
Thow sayis, Lord, lovit mocht ye be
that formed and maid mankind of me.
Thow coft me on the haly croce
And lent me body saull and voce,
And ordanit me to heavinnis bliss
Wherefore I thank the Lord of this;
And all our hallowaris lovit be,
to pray to them to pray to me,
and keep me fra that fellon fae
and from the syn that saull wald slay.
Thow Lord for thy bitter passioun in
to keip me from syn and warldlie schame
and endless damnation.
Grant me the joy newer will be gane,
Sweit Jesus Cristus, Amene.

It will be immediately obvious that the above is not
a "devlish prayer", but a thoroughly Christian rhyming
vernacular version of the Creed. Having ascertained that the
patient was going to live, Agnes would then proceed to recite
her healing prayer:

All kindis of illis that ever may be
in Crystis name I conjure ye.
I conjure ye baith mair and les
with all the vertewis of the mess.
And rycht sa, be the naillis sa
that nailit Jesus and na ma.
And rycht sa, be the samyn blude
that reikit owre the ruithful rude;
Furth of the flesch and of the bane,
I conjure ye in Godis name.

Here Agnes is ordering the sickness to depart from the patient and go into the earth, in Christ's name, by the virtues of the mass, and in God's name. It is also worth mentioning that Agnes's method of healing sick livestock was to strike the animals on the back while chanting "Ave Maria". It will be obvious that however well-intentioned Agnes might have been, the recitation of the Catholic Creed and appeals to Mary and the virtues of the Mass would not endear her to Scotland's still relatively new Protestant establishment, for whom the Mass was indeed almost equivalent to "devlishness".

We are used to think of witches as "mumbling magic words", and we have no way of knowing how Agnes delivered her prayers, but they may well have been dramatic performances of stunning intensity. A touch of melodrama would certainly have helped along a healing process based on psychology. The more a patient believes that the cure will be effective, the more it is likely to be so, and the more the patient believes that he will recover, the more his recovery is likely.

We find Agnes curing Robert Kerse in Dalkeith by taking his sickness upon herself, and holding it fast until morning with much groaning and the appearance of great agony. In the morning she cast the sickness out of herself into the alleyway outside the house, so that a dog or a cat might get it. (Unfortunately, the sickness apparently landed on one Alexander Douglas, who wasted away with it and died.) Agnes's performance in Robert Kerse's house seems very like a piece of theatre designed to impress the patient and his family, thereby boosting both the healing process and Agnes's reputation. Similarly, when Agnes was summoned to heal the laird of Edmondstone's mother, she frightened the daughters of the family out of their wits by raising the black dog Eloa out of the well in the garden, and sending it off howling over the garden wall. Agnes didn't waste time on the old lady, who she said was going to die, but her little trick with the "spreit" from the well would ensure that the young ladies remembered her for the rest of their lives.

Although Agnes's activities centred round healing, she was not above using her powers to do harm if necessary. When the Gudewife of Galashiels refused to pay her for services rendered, Agnes caused her to take a fit of madness during which her tongue shot out and swelled up horribly. When Barbara Napier, an Edinburgh lady, was wronged by a man named "Archie" - her husband's name was Archibald Douglas – Agnes made her a wax image to be melted in front of the fire, with the intention of causing Archie to pine away. Fatefully, Agnes also seems to have been mixed up in a scheme to ruin David Seton of Foulstruther by laying cord with pieces of glass braided into it where Seton was expected to pass. The plotters miscalculated, however, and the ruination landed not on Seton, but on a poor ploughman and his daughter. There were two David Setons, father and son. The elder was Baron Baillie of Tranent, and the proprietor of Foulstruther in the neighbouring parish of Ormiston might have been his son, or the Baron Baillie himself.

However generally benevolent most of Agnes's activities might have been, and however loudly and frequently she appealed for God's back-up for these undertakings, there was, as previously mentioned, no doubt in the minds of the Authorities where Agnes's powers came from. As far as the Kirk and the Law were concerned, all supernatural power involved in healing, magic, and sorcery derived from the Devil, even if it appeared to be used beneficially. It is not surprising, therefore, to find the Synod of Lothian and Tweeddale moving to investigate Agnes in April 1589. The Synod was an administrative layer of the Church of Scotland. The highest administrative level was the General Assembly; next came the Synods; then the Presbyteries, and finally at parish level, the Kirk Sessions. Each of these strata also had powers as church courts. The power to actually put a suspect on trial for witchcraft was the preserve of the secular courts, but the Kirk was entitled, indeed expected, to investigate suspected witchcraft in an information-gathering capacity.

A complaint was aired at the Synod meeting on 1st April 1589 that the Presbytery of Haddington had not called in Agnes Sampson for questioning, although she was suspected of witchcraft and lived within the bounds of the presbytery. A Synod meeting in September noted that Agnes had still not been called in, and the Synod criticised Haddington Presbytery for its negligence. On 5th May 1590 it was reported that some moves had been made against Agnes, and on 7th October Haddington Presbytery reported that they had made a start with her. Synod insisted yet again that Haddington must take her case forward. Accustomed as we are to hearing stories of the Kirk's bloodthirsty enthusiasm for hounding witchcraft suspects to a horrible death, we may find Haddington Presbytery's lackadaisical approach surprising. But then, although Agnes was a particularly notorious Wise Wife, traditional healers and practitioners of folk magic had always been part of the rural scene, and in spite of the demands of the law, a blind eye was usually turned, unless Wise Wives unwisely stuck their heads too far above the parapet, or unless a chorus of complaints that "something must be done" became too loud to ignore.

However, out of the blue, a catastrophic turn of events exploded onto the scene which made Haddington's foot-dragging irrelevant. The story was given the full "shock-horror" treatment in a contemporary English pamphlet "Newes from Scotland" which deliberately dwells on the more sensational aspects of the affair, and includes much which can only be pure fiction. What now confronted the authorities was not only the revelation that witches were apparently wreaking unchecked havoc in East Lothian, but also the details of a diabolical plot to kill the King by magical means. This all began, "Newes from Scotland" informs us, when David Seton, the Baron Baillie of Tranent, began to suspect his servant Geillis Duncan of witchcraft. As Baron Baillie, Seton was the local magistrate. He had Geillis locked up and interrogated. Perhaps Seton had got wind of the previously mentioned attempts to harm him by magic. Certainly, the voluminous official records mention that John Cockburn, a neighbour of Seton's, had promised to pay one Donald Robeson to go to Agnes Sampson for help to ruin David Seton, and we have already heard of Agnes's attempts to do so with enchanted cords and pieces of glass.

Early 17th Century legislation forbade the torture of witchcraft suspects without the express permission of the Government. In 1590 there were no such obstacles, and under Seton's brutal interrogations Geillis Duncan confessed to witchcraft and was duly imprisoned in Edinburgh for further interrogation. She began naming names, and several of her acquaintances were also pulled in for questioning. They in turn named other names, and a multitude of witnesses and suspects was flushed out, including the young schoolmaster of Prestonpans, two ladies of the Edinburgh gentry, and Agnes Sampson.

Central to the various confessions and statements was a grand convocation of witches which had met at North Berwick kirk in the autumn of 1589. Different witnesses give differing and conflicting accounts of the meeting, and indeed different dates. Some even mention two North Berwick meetings, possibly as a result of pressure from interrogators trying to reconcile conflicting accounts. However, the consensus seems to be that there was a meeting of around a hundred witches at North Berwick kirk at Hallowe'en. They danced and sang in the churchyard to the sound of the jews-harp, dug up corpses to obtain body-parts to make into magic powders, and listened to a sermon preached from the pulpit by the Devil in the shape of a man. The sermon allegedly contained uncomplimentary remarks about the King, and afterwards the Devil stuck his bare backside over the pulpit for the congregation to kiss. Agnes Sampson confessed to having attended this get-together, arriving on horseback escorted by her son-in-law John Couper. One might wonder what the douce inhabitants of North Berwick were doing while their ancient place of worship was thus desecrated. One might also wonder whether the meeting (if it took place at all) was quite as large and spectacular as it was painted. All the same, if a venue had to be chosen for some sort of witches' Extraordinary General Meeting with delegates travelling from a distance, North Berwick was an excellent choice, as the hill behind the burgh, Berwick Law, is a prominent landmark clearly visible from Edinburgh and much of Midlothian, and unmistakable from most of East Lothian.

The King, James VI, was newly married. However, his efforts to attain that happy state had been fraught with difficulty. A marriage had been negotiated between James and Anne, the fourteen year old daughter of the King of Denmark. The couple were duly married by proxy at Kroneborg castle in Denmark on 20th August 1589, with George Keith the Earl Marischal of Scotland standing in for James at the ceremony. A Danish fleet set sail for Scotland to carry Anne to her royal husband, but storms and leaking ships forced the fleet to seek shelter in Norway, which was then a Danish possession. A further attempt in October was again frustrated by storms. Anne decided to spend the winter in Oslo, and James decided to join her. After a stormy crossing, James was married in person to his young queen in Oslo on 23rd November. In late January 1590 the royal couple arrived in Denmark and went through yet another ceremony. They set sail for Scotland on 26th April and arrived in Leith after weathering another unpleasantly rough passage.

On 4th July 1590 the English ambassador in Edinburgh observed in a letter to Lord Burghley that news from Denmark had revealed that half a dozen witches had been arrested in Copenhagen on suspicion of having delayed Anne's crossing to Scotland, and of having attempted to prevent King James's return home. It seems very likely that it would be this piece of news which suggested to the authorities in Scotland that some similar plot might have been cooked up on this side of the North Sea. After all, raising storms was believed to be one of the perennial activities of witches, and some very interesting information was being wrung from some of the "North Berwick" witchcraft suspects. The grand get-together in that town had been around the time when the royal marriage was being bedevilled by storms at sea, and some of the suspects were mentioning attempts to sink at least one ship in the Firth of Forth by magic.

Efforts to get to the bottom of this intensified in November and December 1590, and the King began to take an interest, attending interrogations in person. He was sceptical about what he was hearing, and intervened in the questioning of Agnes Sampson, saying that she was contradicting herself, and he insisted that she should tell the truth. However sceptical he had been before, something in this interview seems to have thoroughly convinced him. The records of this interrogation show that Agnes confessed that the Devil foretold a storm at Michaelmas (29th September) to her, and that great harm would be done at sea and on land. She also confessed that the Devil had told her that the King would have great difficulty reaching home, and that the Queen would never get there unless the king fetched her. She also confessed to have been involved in the sinking of a ship off North Berwick. Although so far there was no mention of plotting against the King - only claims of foreknowledge of the storms that disrupted his wedding plans – there was certainly food for thought amongst Agnes's confessions.

According to "Newes from Scotland" James scoffed at Agnes's confessions and accused her of lying, and Agnes then offered to prove that she was telling the truth. There is no mention of this either in the records of her interrogations, or in the record of her trial, but according to "Newes from Scotland" she took James aside and told him the exact words that had passed between him and his bride on the first night after their marriage in Oslo. This made such an impression on James that from then on he accepted the confessions of the suspects without demur. This successful demonstration of Agnes's occult powers – if it ever happened – indeed seems most impressive. But need the knowledge have been obtained by occult means? Remember, Agnes lived at Keith, a stone's throw from the East Lothian residence of the Earl Marischal of Scotland, who had been entrusted with all the King's wedding arrangements. The Earl Marischal had various other houses and castles up and down the country, but after his return from Scandinavia he would surely have been overseeing the finishing touches to his new East Lothian mansion, and is very likely to have been present there at least some of the time. It would be hardly surprising if he had taken a servant or two with him to Scandinavia, nor would it be surprising if his servants picked up titbits of gossip from the young bride's maids or other servants while they were there. We might imagine something particularly salacious or amusing overheard by one of the Queen's personal attendants in the royal bedchamber, or possibly even confided by the Queen to a favourite. This is then whispered through the servants' hall, picked up by the Earl Marischal's attendants, and brought back to Keith where it is bandied about before being tucked away in Agnes Sampson's capacious memory in case it is ever needed. All this of course is nothing but conjecture, but it serves to show how words murmured in confidence in Norway have no need of the occult to wing their way across the North Sea to East Lothian. Nor does the fact that James and Anne apparently communicated in French make any difference. All we need are one or two bilingual human links in the chain of whispers.

If indeed the story in "Newes from Scotland" is true, and Agnes was unable to resist the temptation to impress the King, it was a fatal mistake. The full power of the state fell upon the unfortunate suspects with pitiless determination. Although the initial confessions had mentioned no such thing, gradually a picture was built up of a satanic plot to kill the King, not only by raising storms, but by roasting a wax image, and by utilising a magical concoction containing the drips from a roasting toad. These treasonous plots had been discussed in various locations, including the great North Berwick gathering and another meeting at Acheson's Haven near Prestonpans. By the time the saga was over droves of witnesses and suspects had been questioned, and around a dozen convicted and executed.

What, you may ask, was the point of all this? Well, we are all familiar with the scenario where modern politicians gain prestige by adopting a vigorous can-do approach to an easy target, while prudently ignoring more difficult issues. Similarly, by taking a high-profile stand against the Devil's work in Scotland, the still relatively new Protestant church was able to show that it would brook no mischief from the enemies of God; and the young King, who until recently had been under the thumb of various mentors and manipulators, was able to show himself as a proactive ruler and doughty Christian champion, against whom even Satan's legions could not prevail. As an added bonus, James was even able to discredit his dashing and ambitious cousin the Earl of Bothwell, who according to some of the suspects, was behind the witches' treasonous conspiracies. Although formally acquitted of witchcraft, Bothwell was eventually forced into exile.

The so-called "North Berwick" witches were thus used as pawns in a political game which sacrificed them to the advantage of their rulers and masters.

Agnes Sampson stood trial in Edinburgh, on 27th January 1591, and was found guilty of witchcraft, for which the mandatory punishment was death. She was strangled at the stake the following day on the Castlehill of Edinburgh, and her body burned to ashes. This operation took ten loads of coals, two bundles of heather, a bundle of broom, six tar-barrels, and two dry barrels. With a payment to the wright for setting up the stake, and the hangman's fee, the total cost was £6-8s-10d. It is probably worth emphasising that in Scotland witches were not burned alive, as is commonly supposed, but were strangled to death before their corpses were consumed by the flames.

It was noted at the time that Agnes "died most penitently for her sins and for abusing the simple people, and renounced the Devil, calling him the 'false deceiver of God's people'. She sought refuge in God's mercy and in Jesus Christ in whom alone she was assured to be safe, like the thief who hung at his right hand."

Agnes Sampson is the archetypal example of the Wise Wife, a native practitioner of traditional magic, who had acquired a considerable reputation, who was considered successful and effective, and who clearly operated for many years unmolested. Agnes's work and methods have been obscured and misinterpreted by 16th century officialdom's belief in diabolic witchcraft, by the false evidence cooked up during the investigations of the "North Berwick" suspects, and by the scurrilous sensationalism of the English scandal-sheet "Newes from Scotland". What a pity she could not have been interviewed by someone more akin to a modern folklorist or social anthropologist, instead of the brutal enforcers of 16th century Scottish criminal law!

Isobel Young

Isobel Young, wife of George Smith, portioner of East Barns, was tried by the Justiciary Court in Edinburgh on 4th and 5th February 1629. Hers is one of the most extensively documented East Lothian witchcraft cases, which is interesting in that it sheds much light not only on witchcraft practices, but on rural life of the period.

Isobel's dittay or formal indictment charged that around Martinmas 1620 she had come to Brand's Mill with a bag of corn, asking for it to be ground. Although the hamlet of East Barns now lies semi-derelict, and the landscape is dominated by a cement works and a nuclear power station, Brands Mill still stands where it did in a pleasant spot by the Brox Burn.

When Isobel arrived at the mill she found a queue of poor folk already waiting with bags of corn to be ground, and the miller, George Sandie, refused to attend to her right away. In a rage, Isobel flung her bag of corn into the hopper of the mill, barging against George as she did so. He overbalanced and fell against the hopper, which collapsed on to the bedding of the millstones along with George and the armful of corn he was carrying, badly damaging the machinery of the mill. In a fury Isobel swore that he would regret his refusal, and declared that his mill would lie idle when he least expected it, and most needed it. When the damage had been repaired, it was found that the mill still inexplicably refused to run. This state of affairs lasted for eleven days, then by fits and starts the machinery gradually began to work as usual. Unfortunately, by this time most of George's customers had taken their business elsewhere, causing him great financial loss.

Brands Mill: Isobel Young, the East Barns witch, fell out with the miller of Brands Mill.

A year later Isobel came again to the mill with grain, and as it was being ground she was asked to pay with a portion of the meal. She refused to use the miller's measure for this, however, and insisted on using her own peck measure. George Sandie objected, saying her peck was short measure, and put aside a quantity of Isobel's meal to pay her dues. Isobel went off in a rage with the meal that had been ground, leaving two servant women in the mill to wait for the rest. The night was excessively stormy with wind and rain, and the Brox Burn was in spate. In spite of this, when Isobel returned to the mill later, she was bone-dry. With what would appear to be typical ill-nature, she took back the small quantity of meal the servants had handed over in return for some ale, and confiscated the bannocks they were baking at the fire. Returning home, she crossed the Brox Burn without a horse although the stream was running so high that a work horse of George Sandie's had only been able to cross with difficulty earlier. It was whispered that she had kept herself dry and crossed the flooded burn by occult means.

Not long after this, George Sandie's landlord evicted him from the mill, and it was rumoured that Isobel had used her supernatural powers to influence the laird. George was left in dire poverty, and heavily in debt.   Some years later, George was still suffering hard times, and attempting to earn a living with a fishing coble. When the migrating herring shoals arrived off Dunbar, he went out to the drave, but "could not get as much as the tail of a herring in his boat", while boats all around were hauling in bumper catches of herring. At one point a shoal passed his boat with the herring leaping out of the water as the gulls gorged themselves on them, yet when George and his crew hauled in their nets they had barely a score of herring to show for their efforts, while all the other boats were fully loaded. When he reached the shore he was advised by a Highlandman that Isobel Young had taken his herring by her devilish machinations, and if he wanted to remedy the matter, he should go to East Barns and ask her three times for God's sake to give him back his fish. This he did, and the next time he took his boat out he got more herring than all the other boats put together. It must be said that during the trial, Isobel's defence lawyer made a very good job of rubbishing this entire sequence of events, and cast grave doubts on George Sandie's character so successfully that Isobel was acquitted of all the points of malefice against him.

Isobel was also accused of conceiving a deadly hatred against her neighbour William Meslet and his wife Margaret Ogil. As a "portioner" farming a part of the lands of East Barns, Isobel's husband George Smith included in his holding a piece of land given to him by George Home of Meikle Pinkerton as a pledge for a debt of 400 merks. William Meslet lent Home enough money to pay his debt and redeem his land, a turn of events which greatly angered Isobel. She threatened Meslet with an evil turn, and swore that not only would he never again have enough money to lay out on land, but he would even lose what land he now possessed.

Sometime after Isobel's outburst she came to Meslet to buy a chalder of wheat. When she entered his barn to load the wheat, she took the kerchief from her head and turned herself round three times widdershins (anticlockwise). Not long after this, sixteen of Meslet's best oxen, and eight of his horses suddenly dropped dead. It was also claimed that as Isobel was loading her wheat in Meslet's barn, two sheep came running over the grain pursued by two of Meslet's dogs. She was most put out by this, and was heard to say the sheep would break their necks. Shortly afterwards one of the sheep did indeed meet with an accident, and broke its neck.

Such was Isobel's hatred of William Meslet, it was said, that she even used a family crisis of her own as an opportunity to work evil against him. When her husband George Smith suddenly collapsed while ploughing, Isobel ran to William Meslet's house for a chair, and had her husband carried home in it. It was thought ominous that he was carried home on Meslet's chair through Meslet's barn, for after the return of the chair Meslet's livestock did not thrive as before, his business deals were unsuccessful, and his worldly wealth began to drain away. Isobel's husband recovered quickly from his illness. It was alleged that with the help of the witch Christian Grinton, Isobel had taken the sickness off her husband and laid it at her barn door, so that it would land on whoever first came that way. This unfortunate victim proved to be William Smith, George's nephew, who as he came in at the barn door apparently saw the firlot measuring tub running around the floor with the wheat in it bubbling up as if in a boiling cauldron. In a fit of insanity, he took Isobel by the throat, shouting that she had bewitched him, and he struck at her with a sword. William seems to have recovered his senses, but swore that if he got the opportunity he would pursue Isobel by law to the death for bewitching him.

Misfortune also fell on William Symsone in East Barns and his family as a result of a childish quarrel between Symsone's son Thomas, and Isobel's son, also Thomas, when they were schoolboys. The two boys were fighting, and William Symsone separated them, reprimanded them, and apparently threatened Isobel's son. This caused great offence to Isobel. She came to Symsone's house, on the pretext of buying some pigs. To the family's horror, she sat down in the doorway and took off her kerchief – her usual behaviour when greeting those to whom she bore ill will. A few days later, according to the Symsones, Isobel passed through their courtyard in the form of a hare (a favourite disguise for shape-changing witches in Scotland). Symsone's daughter Margaret had apparently joined in the fight between the two Thomases by nipping Isobel's son's leg. After Isobel's visit in the guise of a hare, the girl fell ill and died.

Symsone's wife Isobell Frude was summoned by the Presbytery of Dunbar to tell what she knew of Isobel Young's witchcraft activities, and was roundly abused on her return. Her face broke out in painful eruptions of the skin from which she could get no relief. She was advised by neighbours to ask

Isobel Young for her health three times for God's sake – one of the usual ways of counteracting witchcraft. After she had done this, her skin gradually cleared until she recovered completely.

The people of East Barns seem to have had long memories. At Isobel's trial she was accused of bewitching Patrick Bryson thirty four years previously, after he had cut her pig's tether. She had ranted and abused him in a towering rage, and flung the cut tether in at his door. As a result, he fell ill and became paralysed down one side of his body, which was left devoid of feeling, and remained so for the rest of his life.

Isobel's malevolence was continued against Patrick's daughter Elizabeth and her husband William Kellie in West Barns. Some years after the tether-cutting incident, Kellie came to Isobel's house with two other men to discuss some business with her husband. As soon as William came in, Isobel took off her kerchief – her usual indication of evil intent – and repeated the action twice more when William had finished his discussions. Soon after this, Kellie's house was burned to the ground along with his barn and barnyard, and all the corn in it.

A year later, William Kellie came face to face with Isobel as he rode through East Barns. She took off her kerchief in her usual manner, and asked him where he was going, but he passed her by without speaking. Isobel called goodbye after him, and suddenly his horse crashed to the ground, knocking William unconscious. His companion John Faa cried out that William had been bewitched, but Isobel clapped him on the shoulder saying, "I'll let him off this time." William struggled to his feet, remounted, and rode home, where he immediately took to his bed. The horse he had been riding died that same night, and William remained bedridden for thirteen weeks.

Around 1607 Isobel fell out with Thomas Home in East Barns and his wife Lillias Knowis, once again over the purchase of a piece of land. Isobel and her husband made an offer for it, but Thomas Home offered 200 merks more. Ever since then, it was claimed, Isobel had done everything she could to ruin him. In a single year 27 animals from his livestock died, and Thomas Home himself then fell ill, racked with pain and wasting away. Eventually he retired to Prestonpans where his brother was schoolmaster.

Among the paperwork for Isobel's trial is a long statement from Home's wife Lillias Knowis. She describes her husband's loss of livestock and his ill health, and how they had moved to Prestonpans. Five weeks before her husband's death she dreamed that she was back in East Barns. From the door of her house she saw Isobel Young and her husband George Smith walking on the roof of Thomas Home's dovecot, which presumably was the sort of substantial stone-built structure which can still be seen in East Lothian to this day. In the dream, Lillias shouted for her husband, but when he came he said he could see nothing. He walked over to urinate against the dovecot wall, and Isobel Young reached down and grabbed at his nightcap. At this, Lillias screamed and woke her husband. Lillias was greatly frightened and disturbed. She was certain the dream was an evil omen and that they hadn't heard the last of it.

The next day their eldest son arrived on horseback from East Barns with news of a curious turn of events. The previous evening, around supper time, all the pigeons in their dovecot, of which there were a great many, came out and sat crowded on the roof before suddenly flying off together. The dovecot was searched in the expectation that a cat or some other animal had got in, but nothing could be found. At once Lillias cried out, "There's the explanation of my dream!" Her husband went over the story of how he had acquired a piece of land that Isobel had her eye on, an how he was aware that she had resented him ever since. Now at last he was convinced she was a witch who had wronged him with her devilry and witchcraft. Thomas Home died soon after this, but Lillias was certain that Isobel was still working evil against her.

Lillias moved back to East Barns, and her steading there burned down in a mysterious fire. She remarried, and one day Isobel came to her house to complain that Lillias's husband had struck a pig of hers. Lillias spoke soothingly to her, as she was afraid of her and did not wish to provoke her. Isobel seemed mollified, and lifted Lillias's little daughter onto her knee and made a fuss of her. Shortly after that, the child, a toddler of eighteen months, fell seriously ill. Eventually, a vagabond woman from England said she could cure the child. She inspected the child's urine and announced that the girl had been bewitched by Isobel Young. After that there was a steady improvement in Lilias's daughter's condition.

There was some pondering among those investigating Isobel's case, over a scar below one of her breasts, which it was thought might be the Devil's mark. It was believed that when witches promised to serve their master the Devil, he would give them a mark somewhere on their bodies as a sort of "membership badge". Among Isobel's trial documents is a statement from Alexander Fortoune, a herbal healer from Duns. He gave evidence that he had treated Isobel on one occasion for a swollen belly, with a potion of oil, vinegar, onions, and mallows; and on another occasion for a pea-sized hole in the flesh under her breast. This he treated with an ointment made of "kemp leaves, bawort roots, curldodies, waybraid leaves, and butter". He observed that when he treated John Fender for a similar complaint, Fender fainted with the pain, but when he asked Isobel if she felt any pain, she replied, "Not at all." Since the Devil's mark was held to be impervious to pain, the implication here is obvious. Fortoune also mentioned that several of Isobel's neighbours were convinced that she could have cured herself as well as any doctor, and had only engaged another healer in an attempt to deny her occult powers. He testified that when he visited her some three months later, Isobel said that she had recovered and was now very well.

There were many other accusations against Isobel, mostly concerning "malifice", that is, causing harm by witchcraft. One interesting exception is the accusation that she had cured cattle disease in her own livestock by burying a live ox in a pit with a cat and some salt. The rest of the cattle were then driven over the spot. This is the sort of ritual which was on the borderline between mere "charming" and actual witchcraft.

At the time of her trial Isobel was over eighty years of age, and had obviously had a reputation as a witch for many decades. Formally accused of witchcraft, she was obliged to give surety to appear for trial in Edinburgh on 20th January 1629. She arrived in Edinburgh on the 13th, and was promptly locked up in the Tolbooth, with no word of her trial coming off. She petitioned the Privy Council to be set free on bail until another trial date was set, and the Lords of Council duly appointed her to appear in fifteen days time.

It is sometimes believed that witchcraft suspects in Scotland were whisked off to the stake after the most perfunctory of trials, or condemned by kangaroo courts of ministers and elders. On the contrary, all suspects were entitled to a proper trial before a jury, and were entitled to a "proloquitor" or representative to speak in their defence. Isobel not only had her three sons to speak for her, but she had the services of David Primrois and Lawrence McGill, two Edinburgh advocates whose lengthy and learned attempts to make nonsense of the charges are meticulously documented in the trial records.

Isobel faced 24 charges of witchcraft, and despite the fact that most of the "assize" or jury came from within a few miles of Dunbar and would certainly be well aware of her reputation as a witch, she was acquitted of half of the charges. Of those of which she was convicted, the jury was unanimous only on the catch-all charge that that she had been "an undoubted witch and sorcerer for forty years", and on the accusations that she had met with the Devil and other witches at Doon Hill, and that she had laid her husband's sickness on his nephew William Smith.

Isobel was sentenced to be taken to the Castle Hill of Edinburgh, to be strangled to death at a stake, and her body to be thereafter burned to ashes. Although it was undoubtedly a harsh fate for an old woman of over eighty to be publicly strangled and burnt, those who like to believe that Scotland was in a constant ferment of witch-hunting, and that the victims were invariably poor and defenceless innocents, might care to ponder over the fact that Isobel had a husband and adult sons, and was prosperous enough to offer to buy land, to keep servants, and to employ two advocates in her defence. Also, in spite of the fact that she was undoubtedly an ill-natured woman who put a lot of people's backs up, and had been widely supposed to be a witch for forty years, she survived unmolested into what in 17th Century Scotland was an exceptionally ripe old age.

Alexander Hamilton

Although the majority of convicted witches were women, they were not exclusively so, and warlocks (or "warlaws" as the 17th Century pronunciation was in East Lothian) were not uncommon. The year 1629 seems to have been one of those years when the authorities felt "something must be done" about witchcraft, and Alexander Hamilton was one of several East Lothian people arrested for the crime in that year.

Hamilton was a native of Prestonpans and worked there as a coal miner in his youth. Later he moved to Northumberland and worked in the collieries there. It would probably have been illegal for him to do this, since colliers in East Lothian at that time were generally bound to the pit where they worked, and could be brought back by force and punished if they left their workplace without the owner's permission. At some point Hamilton seems to have been pressed into military service, and there is mention of him having been in Sweden. Latterly he lived a roving life as a beggar in East Lothian and Berwickshire, and came under suspicion of practising witchcraft. In the hope of avoiding arrest he again crossed the Border into Northumberland. At the time of his trial he was said to be about sixty years of age, and so must have been born around 1570. He is described in a statement among Isobel Young's trial records as a "venomous warlock".

He was arrested at "Killene Mure" three miles from Newcastle under a warrant from the Scottish Privy Council, as a result of the efforts of George Home of Manderston. It has been shown recently in a study by Louise Yeoman that Home was almost certainly using Alexander Hamilton to blacken his wife

Helen Arnot's character with accusations of witchcraft. After Hamilton's arrest Home had him locked up in Berwick, then brought him to the tollbooth of Duns where he was questioned and made a confession. He admitted to having been at several witch meetings in Berwickshire, including one in Duns where the Devil had sex with all the women present. This feat was then emulated by one John Smyth who "usit them all behind and raid them lyk beastes". He also described a meeting on Coldingham Law where Manderston's wife Helen Arnot was present and asked the Devil for help to kill her husband. Following the Devil's advice she dug up a grave and removed the hand from a corpse. The hand was placed in a corner of Home's garden in Berwick where he was in the habit of going every day. On another occasion she had put a dead foal in his stable. Both of these acts were done in the hope that Home would be the first to see the enchanted objects. If so, he would die.

Hamilton later claimed under questioning in Edinburgh that a servant of Home's came to him in Berwick and urged him to say whatever his master told him to say. The business of the dead man's hand had been first suggested by Home himself, and when Hamilton denied any knowledge of it, Home had put him in irons and took him to Duns. On the way, Home's servant again urged him to say what his master wanted him to say, saying that if he did so, Home would be good to him and take care of his children. Hamilton obliged, and confessed "certain things" as requested. The Lords of Council had ordered that Hamilton was to be imprisoned in the tolbooth of Haddington until arrangements could be made to deliver him into the keeping of the provost and baillies of Edinburgh. According to Hamilton, on the way from Duns to Haddington Home personally pressed him to stand by the statements he had made, promised again to be good to him and take care of his children, and went so far as to show his benevolence by giving him a few shillings.

By 15th August 1629 Hamilton was in custody in Edinburgh, where he was closely questioned over the next five months,

Ugston: Alexander Hamilton first met the Devil on the hill behind Ugston.

making a lengthy confession of his crimes and naming large numbers of people as being guilty of witchcraft.

He claimed to have met the Devil around Michaelmas 1624 on the hills above Ugston, while he was on his way from Nunland (now Huntington) to Haddington. The Devil appeared to him as a black man dressed all in black, with a wand in his hand. Hamilton promised to serve the Devil on condition that he would never be allowed to lack food, clothing, and money. He then made so bold as to ask the Devil for some money, but met with a refusal. However, the Devil arranged to meet him again a few days later in the Garleton Hills between midnight and one o' clock in the morning, and promised to give him some money then. When Hamilton kept this appointment the Devil appeared riding on a black horse. After Hamilton had renounced his baptism and promised again to serve the Devil as his bondsman, the Devil gave him four shillings sterling in English money. Alexander Hamilton was carrying a stick, and the Devil explained that if Hamilton ever wanted to consult him, he was to strike the ground three times with his stick, saying, "Rise up, Foul Thief!". Hamilton claimed that when he performed the ritual as described the Devil would appear sometimes as a crow, or sometimes as a cat, a dog, or some other animal, and he would answer Hamilton's questions. In return, Hamilton would offer him a loaf, or a dead cat or dog, or whatever animal came to hand.

Hamilton apparently had a grudge against John Cockburn, the Provost of Haddington. The Devil told him to take three ears of corn out of each of the stacks in the provost's barnyard, then take them to the Garleton Hills and burn them. At the time, Cockburn had a batch of corn drying in a kiln, and as a result of Hamilton's efforts it was all burnt up.

Thomas Home in Clerkington fell seriously ill after a beggar woman laid an enchanted thread at his door. The witchcraft had been intended for Home's father, who had struck the woman, but it had landed on Thomas instead. Alexander Hamilton promised to cure him. He raised the Devil in the form of a crow at the Clerkington Burn. The Devil told him to mix heart-fat, camomile oil, and oil of animal fat, and rub Thomas with it using a woollen cloth. Hamilton had brought along a cat which he had killed with a stone, and after receiving the information he had sought, he threw the cat to the Devil, who vanished away with it. When the cure was applied as instructed, Thomas Home recovered.

Other victims of Hamilton's vindictiveness, according to his own confession, were Lady Ormiston and her daughter. When he was begging for food at the gate of Ormiston Hall, Lady Ormiston's daughter had driven him off, crying, "Away, you custroun carl (layabout)! You'll get nothing here!" He was later approached by three women who also had a grudge against Lady Ormiston, and they met together in Saltoun Wood. Hamilton was given a ball of blue thread, and instructed to lay a piece of it in front of the gate at Humbie House where the Lady and her daughter were staying at the time. This he did, while the women whispered certain words whispered to them by the Devil. A short time after that both Lady Ormiston and her daughter died.

How much trust we can put in Alexander Hamilton's confessions is illustrated by the following events described in the records of Alexander's interrogation. One of the women Hamilton had named as being prominent in the conspiracy against Lady Ormiston was Agnes Allan from Saltoun. In prison, in the presence of he Lord Advocate and the Lord Justice Depute, two women in turn were brought to him, and he was asked to look at them carefully and say whether he knew them. He was vague, and thought he might have seen them before, but was positive that neither of them was Agnes Allan, whom he said he would recognise by a reddish mark on her face. So sure was he that neither of the women was Agnes Allan, that he affirmed that he would be happy to be quartered alive if either of them turned out to be Agnes! He was then informed that one of the women was indeed Agnes Allan, whom he had patently failed to recognise. Hamilton then was forced to admit that he was unable to tell whether or not she was the woman with whom he had conspired against Lady Ormiston. Agnes, on her part, swore that she had never seen Hamilton until she had been confronted with him that day.

Hamilton named several other women as being guilty of witchcraft, and at least some of them were questioned and confronted with him. Proceedings against them do not seem to have been taken further, however. It looks rather as if Hamilton, in a desperate attempt to appear cooperative, was simply giving any names that came to mind; or perhaps, knowing the inevitable outcome of the investigations, he was trying too stave off his trial and execution for as long as possible. He also denounced John Hog and his wife Margaret Nicolson, who lived at Markle near East Linton, claiming that they had invited him into their parlour, given him ale to drink, and asked him if he was one of "the Society". Hamilton admitted eventually that he was indeed a member, and accompanied them a few days later to a meeting with the Devil in a hollow between two hills near Markle. At a subsequent meeting in the hollow, Hog and Hamilton considerately turned their backs while the Devil, in the shape of a black man, had sex with Margaret. Afterwards they returned to Hog's house, where there was a fiddler present, and they ate, drank, and danced till dawn, when Hamilton went off to sleep in the outhouse he was in the habit of occupying. All this was of course strenuously denied by John Hog and his wife, and although they were interrogated at great length in Edinburgh, and had grave suspicions raised against them by some of their neighbours, they were eventually released under caution to appear for trial if required. There is no record of any such trial, so it can probably be assumed that the authorities came to the conclusion that Hamilton's accusations against the Hogs were the product of his fertile imagination.

Alexander Hamilton was tried by the Court of Justiciary in Edinburgh on 22nd January 1630. Since he had already confessed his guilt, the trial was little more than the legal prelude to his execution. The jury duly found him guilty. Interestingly, although he testified in court to the truth of most of his confession, Hamilton declared that everything he had said about George Home of Manderston's wife was untrue, and only hearsay that had been passed to him by one John Neil in Tweedmouth. He also swore that nothing he had said about her had been at the instigation of her husband; a statement which we might well believe was just as untrue as his former accusations against Manderston's lady. Hamilton was condemned to be strangled at the stake on the Castle Hill of Edinburgh, and his body thereafter to be burnt and consumed to ashes – a sentence which would no doubt be carried out within a day or two, as was the usual custom.

Hamilton was no doubt an unsavoury character; scraping a living by begging, using charms to counteract witchcraft and cure disease, and extracting alms by threats of malefice. He apparently had no qualms about denouncing the innocent, and seems to have been happy enough to put Lady Manderston's life in danger when he thought it might save his skin. Apart from perjury, however, his crimes seen to have been of a fairly petty nature, and the impression we are left with is of a rather sad character, used and framed by the unscrupulous laird Manderston, then brutally discarded. Unfortunately for Hamilton, although the authorities obviously decided that his accusations against others were a tissue of lies, they seem to have found it expedient to believe what he testified against himself.

Alexander Sinclair

Alexander Sinclair, also known as Alexander Hunter, was denounced by William Davidson from Saltoun, another warlock tried and executed for witchcraft in December 1628. Sinclair was also described as a "notorious witch" by Bessie Littil, a Longniddry woman who was condemned and burnt around the same time.

George Sinclair's "Satan's Invisible World Discovered", published in Edinburgh in 1685, identifies "Sandie Hunter" as the notorious warlock nicknamed "Hatteraik". It is obvious from some of his remarks that at times George Sinclair is confusing Hunter/Sinclair with his contemporary Alexander Hamilton, and an entry in Haddington Presbytery minutes for 7th November 1628 seems to indicate that "Hatteraik" was in fact Alexander Sinclair's betrayer William Davidson.

According to Davidson, Susanna Sinclair, the elder Lady Samuelston, had consulted with him about arranging the ruin of her brother with whom she had quarrelled. He refused to get involved, and she turned to Alexander Sinclair instead, who obliged by "laying some devilry or witchcraft" around her brother's house at Herdmanston. Lady Samuelston also apparently sought Sinclair's aid to dispatch her ailing husband. She took Sinclair into her husband's bedroom, where he put on one of the sick man's shirts and took it away. What he then did with it is not mentioned in the records, but shortly afterwards Lady Samuelston's husband died.

The Longniddry witch Bessie Littil claimed that she had first made Sinclair's acquaintance when he sent a girl to her to ask for money. Bessie refused to give her anything, and said she had no money. Sinclair sent the girl back again to Bessie with the message that he knew she had a five-merk piece in her chest, wrapped in a cloth. Bessie was rather taken aback by this, as she thought no-one knew about her little nest-egg but herself.

Sinclair displayed the same knowledge of private financial affairs when he came to the house of John Heres in Haddington. Heres had been gravely ill for a long time with some sort of wasting disease. Sinclair, calling himself Seaton, turned up at the Heres household claiming to be a skilful physician, and saying he would be able to heal Heres if he was given one of his shirts. After a week he would return with the shirt and cure the patient. This procedure was in fact quite common, and was used both in diagnosing the disease and in effecting the cure. Agnes Sampson, for example, claimed to be able to get to the root of a health problem by sniffing the patient's linen; and enchanting a shirt, perhaps by washing it in south running water, would restore the owner to good health. Enchanting a shirt could also bring misfortune upon the owner, and we have already seen how Sinclair supposedly brought about the death of Lady Samuelston's husband by taking away one of his shirts. Sinclair may well have intended to work some kind of magic upon Heres's shirt. On the other hand, he may simply have intended to steal it! However, he was not given the opportunity. Heres refused to co-operate, calling Sinclair a witch, and declaring that if he could effect a cure, he could only manage it by using charms and witchcraft.

Before Sinclair left, Heres's wife Elizabeth, perhaps feeling sorry for him, offered him bread and something to drink. He refused her offer, and demanded money instead. When she told him that she didn't have any money he contradicted her, saying that he knew she had a gold five-merk piece and a double pistolet (a foreign gold coin). He also informed her that her husband had gold that she didn't know about, for he had four double angels wrapped in a napkin under his pillow. (The double angel was an English coin bearing the figure of the archangel Michael.) Her husband would not live much longer, he added, and in fact would be dead within a week. Elizabeth swore before the baillies of Haddington that her husband did indeed turn out to have the coins as described by Sinclair, and died as foretold before a week was out.

On another occasion Sinclair came to the house of Adam Nicholson in Longniddry demanding food. Nicholson's wife Isobel Turnbul offered him half a loaf of grey bread. "Grey" bread was coarse inferior bread, usually made from rye. Sinclair haughtily refused the grey bread, and demanded white bread. Isobel quite reasonably pointed out that her reapers working hard in the harvest field were supplied with nothing but grey bread – the inference presumably being that if grey bread satisfied those working hard for a living, it was certainly good enough for a vagabond like Alexander Sinclair. He took grave offence at this, and marched off in high dudgeon.

As soon as Sinclair left the house, Isobel collapsed to the floor where she lay apparently lifeless. Her neighbours came running but were unable to revive her. They pursued Sinclair and brought him back to the house, no doubt because they suspected that Isobel was the victim of Sinclair's witchcraft, and that as the perpetrator of the malefice he was best placed to undo it.

Sinclair instructed the neighbours to bring the whisky he knew they would find in Isobel's cupboard. When she was given a little of this, she immediately recovered. As she did so, a greyhound passing through the room fell down dead on the spot, as did an ox of Isobel's yoked for ploughing, at the same instant. It would be obvious to all present that the sickness had been taken off Isobel and laid on the unfortunate animals.

About a year after these events, Sinclair had the effrontery to turn up at Isobel's door again, expressing amazement that she was still alive, for, he said, she'd had five evils laid upon her, and it was astonishing that she seemed to have been protected from them. He prophesied that she would go far away, as far as Ireland, but would come back again. Isobel told Sinclair's prosecutors that she had indeed gone to live in Ireland for many years before deciding to return.

It was of course part of the stock-in-trade of the wise wife and wandering warlock to be familiar with all the gossip and scandal of the countryside, to keep an ear to the ground for whispers of secrets and hints at future plans, and to marry this with inspired guesswork and shrewd psychology. The ability to foretell the future and see what was carefully concealed were attributes claimed by any self-respecting practitioner of traditional magic, but there was not necessarily much of the supernatural involved.

Sinclair's acquaintance Bessie Littil claimed that he kept a bee in a tin box which he fed each day with three drops of his own blood. Every year, she said, Sinclair would go to Norham in Northumberland to renew his contract with the Devil, and to get a new bee. This may have been a flight of fancy on Bessie's part, but it would not be in the least surprising if Sinclair did indeed carry a bee around with him, hinting at its diabolical origins and describing its unusual eating habits. The bee would be suspected to be a spirit helper, like Agnes Sampson's black dog Eloa, or the various beasts which appeared when Alexander Hamilton struck his stick on the ground. Sinclair's bee would be discussed with unease or even awe, and would be a useful enhancer of his reputation as a man possessed of paranormal powers.

Alexander Sinclair was tried in Haddington on 3rd April 1629. There were two ways to put a witchcraft suspect on trial in Scotland. One was before the High Court of Justiciary, and the other was before a trial by Commission. Trial by Commission involved a group of local pillars of society getting together to petition the Privy Council for permission to set up a special one-off local court to try the suspected witch. If satisfied that they had a case, the Privy Council would grant permission to the "Commissioners" to appoint court officials, call witnesses, call a jury, and nominate a judge or judges from among their own number. It is usually reckoned that a suspect had a better chance of acquittal in the High Court, where the jury would usually be fifteen Edinburgh tradesmen, than in a court set up by commission, where the jury would consist of fifteen men from the neighbourhood, who would be all too familiar with the reputation of the accused.

The Commissioners in Sinclair's case were Sir Robert Hepburn of Adniston, Sheriff Principal; George Hepburn of Alderston, Sheriff Depute; James Cockburn, Provost of Haddington; and three baillies of the burgh of Haddington. The "chancellor" or foreman of the jury was Thomas Bane from Longniddry. Sinclair was found guilty of witchcraft and condemned to be conveyed with his hands bound behind his back, by William Allat, hangman of Haddington, to the ordinary place of execution, strangled to death at a post, and his body thereafter to be burnt to ashes.

The "ordinary place of execution" for condemned witches in Haddington was "the Sands", on the banks of the River Tyne at the east end of the town (now a pleasant leafy residential back street with an art/craft gallery). William Allat or Elliot was a Borderer who had been found guilty of stealing sheep from Letham, outside Haddington. He was offered the choice of either being hanged, or of taking up the vacant post of hangman of Haddington. William made the obvious choice and served the burgh of Haddington for many years. Burgh hangmen, incidentally, were often known by the euphemism of "lokman". This has nothing to do with locks and keys, however, but refers to the "lok" (small quantity or handful) of oatmeal which the hangman was allowed to take from every sack of meal displayed for sale on market days.

Jean Craig

It is a misconception that the Kirk and Law in Scotland were busily conducting a never-ending witch-hunt throughout the 17th Century. There were in fact periods of several years in which witchcraft prosecutions were few and far between; when the authorities seemed to turn a blind eye to the ongoing practice of traditional magic. Some parishes in Scotland – indeed, some in East Lothian – seem to have produced no convicted witches whatsoever. On the other hand, it cannot be denied that there were occasional witchcraft panics when the authorities seem to have been galvanised into action by the conviction that things had been allowed to slide too far, and that "something must be done". These were times when it was very dangerous to be a practitioner of folk magic or an eccentric curmudgeon with antisocial attitudes and habits.

There was no more dangerous time to be a dabbler in the occult than in 1649-50. Civil war had raged in England and Scotland, the King had been imprisoned and beheaded, and Oliver Cromwell had taken power in England. In Scotland the Government was in the hands of a hard-line caucus of fanatical Presbyterian "Covenanters" whose aim was to establish their vision of the Kingdom of God on earth, here in Scotland. All enemies of God had to be rooted out, and among the most obvious of those were Satan's allies and servants, the warlocks, wise wives, and witches. Unfortunately for these pariahs, they were usually easier to lay hands on and bring to book that such other enemies of God as Catholics, Episcopalians, and Royalists in general.

The result was an explosion of arrests, interrogations, trials, and executions, far beyond any of the other outbreaks of Scottish witchcraft persecution, and which ended only with Cromwell's rout of the Covenanting army at Dunbar in 1650 and Scotland's incorporation into his republican "Commonwealth".

One of the early victims of the 1649 panic was Jean Craig from Tranent, the wife of William Steill, a coal miner. In late March and early April she had been detained in the tollbooth of Tranent, and questioned by the minister, and the local magistrate, the Earl of Winton's baron baillie. On April 20th 1649, the Committee of Estates, which was effectively ruling Scotland at the time, ordered that a judge should be sent to Tranent to examine Jean Craig, against whom several allegations of witchcraft had been lodged, and also administer justice on her if necessary. A week later, Jean went on trial before what was in effect a special sitting of the High Court of Justiciary, convened outwith its usual location in Edinburgh.

In Jean, we seem to have someone carrying on a family tradition, for she was the daughter of a convicted witch, Beigis Wallace from Prestonpans, who had been put to death there for witchcraft around 1627. Shortly before this sad event, Jean's husband's sister Agnes Steill had been pregnant. She claimed that Jean and her mother had pestered her to let them have the child when it was born. Apparently, before her execution, Beigis confessed that they had intended to offer the child to the Devil. According to Agnes Steill, when the baby was born Jean had rubbed it all over with three enchanted stones she had got from her mother, as a result of which the child wasted away and died. Agnes had another six children after that, but never managed to produce breast-milk to feed them – the result, she claimed, of Jean's ill-will against her. Not only that, but Jean had conjured up strange uncanny beasts "like pups" which ran around Agnes's house night after night, eventually causing her husband and one of her sons to fall ill, and pine away "in great anguish and pain" till they died.

Another accusation against Jean was that about twelve years before her trial she had caused a woman by the name of Beatrix Sandilands to go raving mad. Jean and her husband had been living in Penston at the time, a mining village about two miles east of Tranent. During the period of evidence gathering leading up to Jean's trial, a request for information was sent from Tranent to the baron baillie of Penston, who was the brother of the laird, Baillie of Lamington. His reply is among the trial papers, and it makes interesting reading. He obviously remembered Jean well, and he begins by saying that she had a very bad reputation, and was known to keep company with witches, particularly Margaret Mathieson and Janet Reid, who had both been burnt at Prestonpans for witchcraft. His outstanding memory of Jean was that she had quarrelled with Beatrix Sandilands at the coal pit at Penston where they both worked. Jean had shouted that she would "see a black sight of her", and then blew in Beatrix's face. Beatrix went mad, to the extent that five or six people were scarcely able to hold her.

Hearing of this, the baron baillie summoned Jean to appear before him, and when she refused to do so, he ordered her husband William Steill to bring her. When she finally came before the baron court, the baron baillie made her go down on her knees and ask her victim's forgiveness, and told her that if Beatrix's health continued to suffer, he would summon Jean again. After that, Beatrix recovered, but when the Laird of Lamington heard about these ongoings he ordered his brother to evict Jean and her husband, which he did. The draft indictment for Jean's trial goes on to describe how Beatrix Sandilands was lying at home bound hand and foot for her own safety, when a great number of cats appeared in the house, leaping and dancing around the fire. When Beatrix's husband John Parkie, picked up a rope to drive them out, they quickly disappeared out through a hole in the wall; but the last one turned and addressed Parkie with a human voice, saying, "Hey, what's wrong with Beatie now?" This incident did not appear in the final version of the indictment, nor did the further accusation that Jean had scattered pieces of raw flesh through John Parkie's house – a common ritual for causing misfortune. Whatever the cause, in spite of her apparent temporary recovery in Penston, Beatrix Sandilands eventually died, and it was the opinion of "the whole parish of Tranent and the country people round about" that Jean Craig was to blame.

Another charge in the draft indictment that never made it into the final version was the accusation that Jean had bewitched a Tranent coal miner named James Cowan who had fallen out with her husband. It was claimed he was cursed with an uncontrollable urge to claw at his skin, particularly his face, till it ran with blood. Cowan also saw visions of Jean appearing by night at his bedside, and he was pulled out of bed and tumbled around the floor by evil spirits which came out from under his bed in the shape of black dogs. His mind had been so unhinged by these experiences that he had taken to hiding under beds or up in the rafters of his house in hopeless attempts to avoid his persecutors. It was also claimed that when Cowan's son broke his leg while at work in the pit, this was also the result of Jean's ill-will and sorcery.

Jean apparently bore a grudge against James Smith, a farmer at Little Fawside to the west of Tranent. It was said that early one morning she walked through Smith's byre and laid a devastating sickness on his cattle. The cows gave blood instead of milk, and the oxen ran mad. The herd-boy employed to look after them disappeared never to be seen again. Not long after that, Jean appeared again at Little Fawside, as one of James Smith's ploughmen was leading out the horses. Jean crossed his path, and addressed the ploughman, saying, "What the devil are you doing, man, up so early in the morning?" Three of the horses afterwards dropped dead, and within a short time the remaining three horses, and the ploughman himself, were also dead.

On 27th April Jean went on trial before the professional judges Colville and Robertoun, and a jury of fifteen, five of whom were from the nearby village of Seton, four from

Longniddry, and four from Winton. One juror was resident in Tranent, and one in Prestonpans. Thus, the entire jury lived within a three mile radius of Tranent, and all would be well aware of Jean's reputation. In any case, Jean had been examined by the witch-pricker John Kincaid, and the Devil's marks had been found. She had also made a partial confession before the minister and baron baillie of Tranent, in which she admitted that she had served the Devil, who had first appeared to her in the form of a cat.

Not surprisingly, Jean was found guilty of sorcery and witchcraft, and it was decreed that on Tuesday 1st May she should be taken to the Muir-brow, strangled at a stake, her body burned to ashes, and all her moveable goods forfeited to the crown.

Penston: A hotbed of witchcraft around 1649.

Margaret Dickson and the Penston Witches

No figure looms larger in the annals of Scottish witchcraft than the Devil himself, and yet in all probability he is an alien import into the world of Scottish traditional magic. The question of where witches in Scotland thought their power came from throws up a variety of answers according to which witchcraft cases are studied. It is clear some practitioners thought they had an inborn gift, while others thought the skills could be learned. Some obviously assumed that power came from the rituals and forms of words they used, while many clearly believed their power came from God. None of these possibilities is mutually exclusive.

In mediaeval Europe, however, the notion grew and flourished in the universities and the upper echelons of the Church that witches and all practitioners of magic derived their power from Satan – a belief which was almost certainly never previously entertained among ordinary folk in Scotland. A grandiose construct of witchcraft theory was built up, claiming witches as the handmaidens of Satan, each of whom had made a personal covenant with the Devil to serve him. It was believed that his servants engaged with sexual activity with their master, and that they would meet regularly with other witches to worship the Devil and to plan evil. These meetings were often held to be hellish orgies, where the participants would drink blood, feast on human flesh, and indulge in vile sexual perversions.

Championed by the Church and the Law, a version of these wild imaginings spread to Scotland, and not only survived the

Protestant Reformation, but was vigorously propounded by the religious and political establishment in their intermittent battles against witches as "enemies of God". James VI in his book "Daemonologie" provided his subjects with a handy list of "things witches do" which was no doubt most useful to interrogators and prosecutors in their search for evidence. Thus, it came to be taken for granted by the Authorities, that those with a reputation for witchcraft were in league with the Devil, and that lesser offenders who used charms and incantations allowed themselves through stupidity and ignorance to be used by Satan as his pawns.

It must be said, however, that Scottish diabolism seems to have been a rather douce and relatively tame variety of Satanism. The Devil did certainly extract a promise from new recruits to serve him, and it was de rigeur for his servants to have sex with their master from time to time, but orgies were almost unheard of, and witch meetings tended to be low-key affairs with little of the foul horror of the Continental "witches' sabbat". Witches might dance, often to a piper, and might have a bite to eat or a drink of ale or wine, and the Devil almost always presided, but many of these meetings read in the records more like good-natured nocturnal picnics than Robert Burns's over-imaginative portrayal of the high-jinks at Alloway Kirk.

Indeed, the Devil himself often comes out in the records as a strangely bland figure, who may sometimes take on the form of a familiar domestic animal, but never appears as a savage beast or monster. He may sometimes appear as a fine gentleman dressed in green, and often as a black man, but most of all he simply manifests himself "in the shape of a man". Nor does he seem to have had much to do, apart from presiding at meetings and fornicating with new recruits.

In the case of Margaret Dickson and her associates we see the tension between the older native "wise wife" tradition of magic and healing, and the insistence of the Kirk and Law that all those involved in the occult must be the Devil's brood.

Considering Margaret and the Penston witches may help us to form an opinion on what substance, if any, there may have been in the diabolic aspects of Scottish witchcraft.

In 1643 Margaret Dickson was living at Nisbet, on the banks of the River Tyne in Pencaitland parish. A man by the name of James Mill lodged a complaint against her with Pencaitland Kirk Session. When he had been ill two years previously, Margaret had offered to cure him by putting him through a hank of yarn; worse, she had made the offer on a Sunday at the time of divine worship. Then, at harvest time in 1642, Mill had caught Margaret's daughter pulling up some of his wheat, and had given her a telling-off. This angered Margaret, and she mocked him for making so much fuss about two or three ears of wheat when there was a time coming when he would lose much more than that. Others had heard her say that she hoped to God Mill would be stabbed in a gutter like his grandfather, and that his children would come to a bad end. Not long after this Mill's livestock were seized with "a kind of trembling disease", and several beasts died. He suspected that Margaret was to blame for this.

When the Session looked into this they found a number of witnesses able to confirm Margaret's reputation for witchcraft. William Baxter had heard her threaten James Mill, and she had said to William himself that she hoped to see Mill go an ill road, and hoped to see him carried home in a barrow by Martinmas.

John Sharp testified that when his daughter was ill, Margaret came to his house and advised him to bake a peck of meal, and take the empty shells of twelve eggs, and lay them with the bread in front of the fire. He was then to lay his daughter behind the fire, go round the outside of the house nine times at midnight, then come in and say, "Rise up, elf, and go back where you should go in the Devil's name, and give me my daughter again." (The implication here seems to be that she believed the girl to be a changeling, and that the "real" child had been spirited away by fairies.) Margaret told him that if the bread and eggshells had gone when he came back into the house, his daughter would recover. If they were still where he had left them, she would not. Margaret apparently admitted this to the kirk session, claiming that an old woman had told her about the ritual. However, she had said three times round the house at ten o'clock, not nine times at midnight.

Another witness, Isobel Johnston, said that Margaret Dickson had attempted to cure her daughter by washing the child's shirt, and the girl herself, twice in south-running water. Margaret had wanted to perform the ritual a third time, but the mother objected as the child was burning with fever. Margaret then advised Isobel that the child was not really her own, but was a hundred years old. Again, the obvious inference is that the child was a changeling. Isobel was to put on a good fire and throw the child into it. (This was in fact the traditional treatment for changelings in folklore. The substituted elf would disappear up the chimney, and the stolen child would be miraculously restored.) Isobel had wisely chosen not to follow Margaret's advice, but had allowed her to bless the child, and herself as well.

What these witnesses carefully omit from their statements, of course, is the fact that Margaret is unlikely simply to have turned up unannounced at their doors, but had in all probability been sent for by the witnesses themselves. Indeed, Margaret said that Isobel Johnston had pestered her "six or seven times in an hour" to fetch burn water to wash her child and offered her sixpence to do so. Note how Margaret claims she was asked to fetch mere "burn" water, rather than the magically potent south-running water she was undoubtedly requested to bring.

Pencaitland Kirk Session referred the case up to the Presbytery of Haddington, and Margaret and her accusers appeared before the Presbytery on 25th April. The witnesses confirmed their previous statements, and Margaret admitted the substance of their claims. She denied, however that she had told James Mill to go through a hank of green yarn, but had told him to wind the yarn round the affected part of his body. She added that when she had advised Isobel Johnston to throw her child in the fire, she had meant her to throw the child on among loose soil.

The Presbytery decided that sufficient indications of witchcraft had come to light to make it worthwhile having a copy of the evidence made to be "sent on". This was the usual procedure in cases of suspected witchcraft. Since a mere church court was not empowered to try cases of witchcraft, the information gathered would have to be passed to a civil magistrate who could then initiate proceedings either to have the suspect tried in the High Court of Justiciary, or make application for a Commission to set up a special local court. It was later noted that the copy had been made, but if it was passed on, nothing more was done about it.

If Margaret Dickson thought she had escaped, however, she was mistaken. As has previously been mentioned, the year 1649 brought in a full-scale witchcraft panic. In normal circumstances, most ministers and kirk sessions were reluctant to believe that any of their parishioners could be guilty of anything so heinous as witchcraft; and dabblers in the occult, and even full-time practitioners of traditional magic were more likely to receive an ecclesiastical slap on the wrist for "charming", rather than find themselves being dragged to the stake by the Haddington "lokman". But in 1649 East Lothian seems to have been in the grip of witch-hunting hysteria, and the least whiff of suspicion could prove fatal.

It is not clear why suspicion fell on the mining village of Penston, where Margaret Dickson was living by 1649. Presumably in the beginning somebody denounced someone else, the Kirk felt bound to investigate, and as the investigation proceeded, more and more names were named, and more and more suspects rounded up for questioning. Penston in 1649 was part of Haddington parish, lying at its western edge, far from the burgh of Haddington itself, and would probably not be troubled often by visits from the minister. On 8th June, nevertheless, four men met in Penston to question two witchcraft suspects there. They were Robert Kerr, minister of Haddington; Thomas Foulis and John Easton, probably kirk elders; and John Baillie, the baron baillie, acting for his brother the laird of Lamington. The unfortunate suspects were Agnes Hunter and Margaret Dickson.

Agnes Hunter confessed to meeting the Devil first in the likeness of a gentleman, secondly in the likeness of a man in green clothes, and for a third time, in the shape of a black man. She renounced her baptism and promised to serve the Devil. She had sex with him, and he asked her to attend a meeting in Thomas Dickson's house in Longniddry. She duly attended the meeting, where food and drink were provided, including a quart of wine. After an hour and a half a further meeting was arranged for the same venue, and the company parted. It was noted that the householder, Thomas Dickson, was unaware of these ongoings, so presumably he was either away from home at the time, or had a large house where high jinks could take place without his knowledge, perhaps in the servants' quarters. A third meeting was arranged for Easter at Penston, where the Devil was to give his servants their "rewards" (whatever they might have been supposed to be), and Agnes Hunter was to be formally enrolled in the "company" the Devil had at Penston. Attending these meetings at Longniddry were Marion Richieson, Margaret Russell, Margaret Richieson, Margaret Staig, and another woman Agnes Hunter did not recognise.

At the Easter Meeting in Penston Agnes met with the Devil, John Dickson, our old acquaintance Margaret Dickson, and Grissell Anderson. As they were gathering together Marion Richieson arrived, greeting the company with, "God speed!" At the mention of God's name the Devil promptly vanished, and the company scattered – presumably without receiving their promised rewards.

Having secured a confession from Agnes, the minister, the baron baillie, and the two elders turned their attention to Margaret Dickson. Margaret declared that she first fell into the Devil's snare about five years previously because of her daughter's ill health. She had spent all her money in attempts to get her daughter cured, and when the girl was a little better, Margaret asked her to go out and gather in the harvest field. The girl refused, and in exasperation Margaret struck her, exclaiming, "You're such a burden to me, I wish that either God or the Devil would part me and you!" At midnight that same night, as if in answer to Margaret's rash appeal, the Devil appeared, came into Margaret's bed, and asked her to become his servant. She was unwilling at first, but the Devil persisted and eventually persuaded her. She had sex with him, renounced her baptism, and promised to serve him. He nipped her right arm, leaving a permanent mark, gave her the witch-name "Marret", and promised her that she would never want.

Margaret had several subsequent meetings with the Devil, including one where he struck her and attacked her viciously because she refused to have sex with him. She attended a witch-meeting in the moor of Gladsmuir, a tract of wild uncultivated country lying between Haddington and the present-day village of Macmerry. The witches danced for an hour, and the Devil lay with Marion Richieson.

After moving from Nisbet to Penston, Margaret was called out by John Dickson, and was taken by him to where the Devil, John Weir, Isobel Murray, Grissell Anderson, and Agnes Hunter had gathered Almost immediately Marion Richieson arrived and scattered the company by wishing them "God speed", as described in Agnes Hunter's confession.

Margaret also mentioned a rather odd encounter from her days at Nisbet. She was sitting with Agnes Broun in Agnes's house when the Devil came in, remarking that he didn't know which of them to turn to. Agnes replied, "Whichever of us you like." The Devil then turned to Agnes, who winked at Margaret, and asked her to leave. As she made to go out, the Devil pulled her back, and joined her hand in Agnes's, telling them both to be good servants to him, and they would not lack their wages.

The business of Isobel Johnston in Nisbet and her sick child was brought up again. Margaret claimed this time that Isobel had been asking her if she thought south-running water would benefit the child. Margaret decided to ask the Devil's opinion, and he told her to fetch the water and give it to the child's mother, but to do no more than bring the water, as it was up to the mother to apply it.

On the following day, 9th June, the Minister and the Provost of Haddington, along with one of the baillies of the burgh, interrogated Isobel Murray, wife of John Weir, meal-maker in Penston. Isobel had been imprisoned in Haddington under suspicion of witchcraft, and on 12th June she was questioned again. She described first meeting the Devil in the shape of a great black dog, and confessed to attending a meeting at Butterdean near Penston where the Devil danced holding Isobel Anderson's hand, and Margaret Dickson sang. She also mentioned the meeting at Penston cut short by Marion Richieson speaking the name of God.

On June 20th, Haddington Presbytery judged the confessions of Margaret Dickson, Agnes Hunter, and Isobel Murray sufficient evidence to apply for a commission for a trial. Parliament granted permission the next day on June 21st, and on the 23rd they were tried in Haddington, along with John Dickson and Marion Richieson. The jury found them guilty unanimously, and they were sentenced to be taken that same day to "the Sands" by the hangman of Haddington, with their hands bound behind their backs. There, about three o' clock, they were strangled to death and their bodies burnt to ashes.

This was not the end of the matter, however, for those named by the condemned witches had then to be questioned, and still others were drawn into the net in the course of the investigations. On July 24th, Helen Fairlie, Barbara Purdie, Helen Lawson, and John Weir were tried, condemned, and executed in Haddington, and on 17th August Margaret Robertson, Margaret Bartilman, Agnes Broun, Janet Burgane, Margaret Paterson, Jean Hunter, and Marjorie Nisbet were likewise tried, and met the same fate at the Sands. Thus, within the space of a couple of months, fourteen people from Penston and the surrounding countryside were put to death for the crime of witchcraft. Many others must have been looking over their shoulders and treading very warily! Up until the early 20th century, the "Witches' Tree" near Penston was still being pointed out as the witches' gathering place.

Now, why, you might ask, did so many presumably sane people confess not only to meeting the Devil (a being considered by most people nowadays to be a figment of the imagination), but to having sex with him? There is a clue in Janet Dickson's records. She was first investigated for magical "wise wife" activities, but these did not lead to a trial. What did lead to a trial and conviction was her confession to meeting and consorting with the Devil, and to attending witch-meetings. Engaging in magical activities where no harm was done could legitimately be considered as mere "charming", and "malefice" or harming by magic was extremely difficult to prove. If, for example, I wish a "black sight" of you and you subsequently go mad, various witnesses might presume that the one caused the other, but it would be well-nigh impossible to prove in a court of law. It was much more effective, therefore, to ignore the magic, and concentrate on extracting a simple confession of consorting with Satan. Ministers, elders, and baron baillies would be well aware of the sorts of things witches were expected to get up to, and would direct their questioning accordingly. Although it was illegal to torture witchcraft suspects after the early years of the 17th Century, extreme psychological pressure, ill-treatment, leading questions, and sheer dogged persistence would usually be enough to extract the desired confession. Once the confession was obtained, the suspect's fate was sealed. Unless she later had the courage to repudiate the confession, her trial was just a formality, as she had already admitted her guilt.

On the other hand, isn't there a very genuine ring to Margaret Dickson's account of the Devil coming into Agnes

Broun's house and wondering which of the ladies to choose? "Whichever you like," said Agnes, and as the Devil turned to her, she winked and asked Margaret to leave. Here we have neither the haughty Prince of Darkness nor the dreadful Beast from the pit of Hell. This is almost a believable Devil.

Janet Bruce

After Oliver Cromwell's overwhelming victory at Dunbar in 1650, Scotland was forcibly incorporated into union with England under Cromwell's republican "Commonwealth" government. An English army of occupation kept order, and a number of witchcraft suspects awaiting trial or questioning seem to have been freed. It has been said that under the Commonwealth a much more enlightened attitude towards witchcraft prevailed in Scotland, the inference sometimes being that this was because of the more civilised outlook of the country's new English masters. Certainly, there was nothing like the holocaust which had been stopped in its tracks by Cromwell's conquest, but it is a mistake to believe that witchcraft prosecutions stopped altogether. In fact, the records show that at least sixteen people from East Lothian alone were executed for witchcraft under the Commonwealth regime. One of those was Janet Bruce from Tranent.

There is no mention of Janet in any of the church records, so it may be that the initial complaints against her were made to a civil magistrate rather than to the minister or kirk session. Janet had been imprisoned in Tranent under suspicion of witchcraft, and on 22nd June 1657 a succession of witnesses appeared to give sworn statements before Andrew Marjoribanks and Robert Hodge, two of the magistrates appointed in East Lothian by the Commonwealth authorities. They were termed "Justices of the Peace", and were presumably intended to replace the baron baillies appointed by local landowners, whose loyalty to the Commonwealth might have been dubious. Several other witnesses appeared a week later on 29th June before Hodge and Sir John Johnston of Elphinstone, another justice of the peace.

Janet was also examined by John Kincaid, a professional witch-pricker, who found four suspected witch-marks on her body. Before several witnesses he inserted a long pin into each of the marks without drawing blood. The supporting paperwork for the case includes a rough drawing of the pin to show its length. If the representation is accurate, the pin, including the head, was 59mm long. It was usual to insert such pins right up to the head. Kincaid declared on his oath that the marks were "of diabolical origin", and signed the declaration with his mark on 30th June.

Janet Bruce was then sent to Edinburgh for trial and imprisoned in the Tolbooth there. Her trial was scheduled for 7th July, but was postponed for some unknown reason, and eventually took place before a jury in the High Court of Justiciary on 4th August, under judges Mosely and Goodear. Her "dittay" or indictment is carefully recorded in the High Court Minute Book, and differs little from the original witnesses' statements. Interestingly, there is no confession, or indeed any statement from Janet herself, and she pled not guilty to all the charges.

The first article of her dittay states that she has been in the service of "Sathan, the enemy of man's salvation" for the past sixteen years. She is accused of entering a diabolic pact, renouncing her baptism, receiving the Devil's mark, laying on and taking off sickness from both humans and animals, and causing many deaths. This is not to say, however, that she or anyone else actually testified to the diabolic pact. It may just have been assumed that since she was a notorious witch, it must be so.

James Melville, a salter from Prestonpans, testified that a year previously he had come into a house in Prestonpans where Janet was drinking with a friend, Elspeth Baptie. Janet had a little black dog which attempted to bite Melville, and he threatened to throw it in the fire. After muttering to herself, Janet told him she would do him a bad turn before long. That very night his salt pan was blown over by the wind, and the contents ruined. This disaster he blamed on Janet. Melville also stated that when Katherine Kniblo, a widow in Prestonpans, asked Janet how she came to know so many different cures, Janet had replied that if Katherine agreed to serve her, she would make her as expert as herself in seven years.

Obviously, then, Janet had a reputation as a healer. This is confirmed by the next charge in her dittay. John Phinnie was a young man whose wife was lame and had been confined to bed for several months. Her mother Marion Faw had heard that Janet was able to cure all kinds of strange diseases, and so Janet was sent for. She undertook to cure Phinnie's wife, and he agreed to pay her £14 for her pains. However, after that, Janet came to Phinnie's wife and announced that unless she was given a gift, she would not be able to effect the cure. When asked what sort of gift she was looking for, Janet told the horrified woman that she must give her a child. Her patient refused indignantly, and Janet made do with taking away some of her clothing. Soon after this, Janet invited Phinnie to supper. When he arrived, she sent her daughter out to buy a mutchkin of wine, and again made the suggestion that Phinnie should give her one of his children to ensure the efficacy of the cure. Phinnie retorted that God had not given him children to be given to the Devil. He refused the proffered supper and left abruptly, and at the time of Janet's trial Phinnie's wife was still no better than before.

Alexander Johnston, another Prestonpans salter, had a son who became paralysed below the waist. He consulted legitimate physicians, spending a lot of money in the process, but the boy grew no better. He came to see Janet in Tranent, and she promised to cure the boy within five days. True to her word, she came to Johnston's house, applied a poultice to the child, and rubbed him with oil. Within five days he was able to stand, and after that grew better every day.

Janet was also sent for by Bessie Ronald, the mother of another sick child. Janet called at the house, took the child on her knee, and carefully measured he child's length with a strip of red velvet. The child recovered and Bessie rewarded Janet with free drink. However, when Janet asked for more, Bessie refused. Janet reminded her that she had done her a good turn, then added significantly, "All the same, if you have the child, I have its measurements."

Janet seems to have been in the habit of stravaiging through the countryside. She was accused of having come to Oxton in Lauderdale two years previously, where she arrived at the home of Marion Hamilton, claiming to be able to cure any disease. Marion said she was troubled with a cyst, and would Janet be able to help? "As God may judge me on the Last Day," replied Janet, "I'll make you as perfect as the day you were born." Marion then rather naively gave her three dollars, and Janet went on her way. One of her neighbours then informed Marion that Janet was a witch. With a male companion, she then set off in pursuit to get her money back. They overtook Janet at Channelkirk, and a struggle ensued where Marion and her friend failed to wrest the money from her, but were left with her plaid. They noticed that some odds and ends seemed to be tied up in a corner of the plaid, and when they went to satisfy their curiosity they found, to their horror, the arm and thigh of a dead child, still fresh enough to be not yet putrified. The identity of the unfortunate child seems never to have been discovered, but if the body parts in question were in fact human, it throws a very sinister light on the earnest requests of Janet Bruce and the other Tranent witch Jean Craig, to be given a child. In some countries of present-day Africa there is an ongoing problem of children being abducted and killed for their body parts which are considered to be powerful ingredients in the making of traditional magic by "witch doctors". Was something similar going on in 17th Century East Lothian, or was Janet merely a grave-robber?

One of the stock Scottish witchcraft beliefs was that witches had the ability to enter houses in defiance of locks and bolts. Janet Bruce's knack of doing the same thing was experienced by Robert Seaton, who had made a deal to sell the fruit from his trees to Janet and her son John Thomson. (This, by the way, would indicate that Janet was, or had been, married to a man named Thomson, although there is no mention of him in the documentation of her trial. We have already seen a brief reference to Janet's daughter.) Half the price of the fruit was to be paid when the bargain was struck, and half when the fruit was picked. After Janet and her son had gathered in the fruit, Seaton and his wife asked several times for their money, without success. Eventually, Seaton had Janet's son John Thomson arrested. A few days later, Seaton's wife Barbara was rudely awakened at midnight by her husband who was sitting up in bed naked, lashing out with his arms. When she had calmed him down he insisted that Janet Bruce and two others had come into the room, seized hold of him in his bed, and pulled his nightshirt over his head. Next morning he set out to confront Janet in her own house, but he was stopped by neighbours, and returned home reluctantly without exacting the revenge he had planned. One can't help thinking that there was not necessarily much in the way of witchcraft involved here, but every likelihood that Janet and a couple of cronies might indeed have slipped into Seaton's house at midnight with the intention of giving him the fright of his life and having a good laugh at the same time.

Janet's readiness to take revenge for perceived injustices was not always so harmless. As we have seen, Janet was in the habit of going off on tours through the countryside, and in 1649 had been "away in the south as was her custom". She had been away for so long, with her house lying empty, that another prospective tenant came to Janet's landlady Margaret Strathearn, enquiring about renting Janet's house. In the course of the discussion Margaret remarked that all the goods in Janet's house were not worth as much as would pay the rent she owed. Unfortunately, the next day Janet came home and berated Margaret for defaming her behind her back. For several nights after this confrontation Margaret was terrified by visions of Janet standing by her bed. Shortly after this, a brood sow of Margaret's fell sick, and probably suspecting that this unfortunate turn of events was Janet's doing, she asked Janet to come and look at the sow. Janet treated the sick animal with a mutchkin of ale and some powder she brought from her own house, saying that the sow had received a "wrong" that had been meant for somebody else. Eventually, she announced that the sow would die - which it did, a few days later. Margaret and her husband made up their minds to get rid of Janet, and when she came to pay her rent on the following term day, Margaret's husband informed her that he had arranged to rent her house to someone else. Janet left without a word, but early next morning she confronted Margaret again, and when she was told that her house had indeed been let to another tenant, she exploded with, "By the bread of God, that will make it the dearest house that was ever built in Tranent!" When Margaret countered with, "I trust you have no power!" Janet let loose a torrent of curses, and swore that she would make Margaret's husband "beshite his breeches for it". True to Janet's promise, Margaret's husband was seized with violent diarrhoea, which continued for a year and a half, as he wasted away in great pain until he died.

Nor was that the only time Janet took revenge for being evicted. At a later date she rented a house from one Robert Sandilands in Tranent. Because of Janet's bad reputation as a witch, Sandilands decided to let her house to another tenant. In a rage, Janet confronted him in his own home, and getting no satisfaction, squatted down in his doorway and urinated on the threshold. When Sandilands protested, Janet swore she would do him an evil turn; nay, she would make him hang himself behind his own bed! But witchcraft was never an exact science. Sandilands himself remained unharmed, but shortly after his contretemps with Janet, one of his children lost the power of both legs, and at the time of Janet's trial, was still paralysed.

Finally, it seems as if a desperate attempt was made by diabolic forces to rescue Janet while she was in custody. While the various witnesses were being interviewed, Janet was being held in Patrick Erskine's house in Tranent. Around midnight, according to James Brotherstanes who was keeping watch over Janet, a rat suddenly seized the candle out of the candle-holder beside her, and darted with it into the thatch above. Soon the whole house was ablaze. Another witness swore that as she was watching the fire, she saw a black horse appear on the top of the burning house, turning this way and that, and beating upon the roof with its hoofs, until it was engulfed in the collapse of the building. Brotherstanes took Janet to his own house, and left her in the care of his wife while he went back to help to fight the fire. As his wife stood in her doorway, at the top of an outside stair, watching the blaze, a raven came swooping over the burning building straight at her face, as if it was trying to fly into her house. She cried out in terror, causing Janet to remark enigmatically that she might well have gone away with the raven.

We may feel a degree of scepticism about rats running around carrying burning candles, and may suspect that it is rather more likely that Brotherstanes was desperately trying to cover up some piece of carelessness or negligence on his own part. It also says much about Janet's reputation that people seem to have been quite prepared to believe she was able to call up demonic rats, ravens, and horses.

As previously mentioned, Janet's trial, originally scheduled for 11th July, was postponed until 4th August. The jury acquitted her of all charges, except that of asking John Phinnie's wife to give her a child, and of having the severed limbs of a child in her possession at Channelkirk. This, of course, is another prime example of how the odds were stacked against witchcraft suspects. All the mumbo-jumbo and macabre nonsense about bewitchings and magic rats have been dismissed, but Janet is still held guilty of witchcraft because she asked for a child (which she never got), and because she was found in possession of body parts which it was assumed she would use for nefarious purposes. There is not even the suggestion that she had actually killed the unfortunate child concerned.

Perhaps there was some doubt in the minds of the authorities as to the justice of the verdict, since it was apparently decided to delay sentencing Janet until 8th October. On that date, however, she was duly sentenced to be taken to the Castle Hill of Edinburgh on 14th October, to be there strangled at a stake, her body burned to ashes, and her possessions forfeited. At least she had not been hustled off to the stake on the same day as her trial, as seems to have been par for the course in pre-Commonwealth days.

John Kincaid

As has already been briefly mentioned, one of the mediaeval academic witchcraft beliefs which made their way to Scotland from continental Europe, was that the Devil would mark the bodies of his servants so that they could be identified as his own. In England, if such marks took the form of protuberant growths, they were often held to be supplementary teats, at which the witch would suckle her "familiars" – imps or evil spirits in the form of small animals. This bizarre belief does not appear to have been common in Scotland, where witch-marks, or "the Devil's mark", seem to have been looked upon more as a sort of membership badge. There is no general agreement as to how the Devil left his mark on his servants' flesh. Many witches confessed to having received the mark, but they differ in accounting for how it got there. Some claimed a mere touch or a kiss produced the mark, but others describe a painful nip. Certainly, if there is any truth behind the theory that witches sported the equivalent of a club badge, and if someone masquerading as "the Devil" did indeed mark new recruits, a forcefully administered nip, perhaps gouging out a piece of flesh, might indeed leave a permanent scar.

The obvious difficulty is that the human body, particularly as it progresses through middle age to old age, is likely to acquire all sorts of scars, blemishes, tags, warts, cysts and tumours – to say nothing of birthmarks or minor disfigurements present from the beginning. Just as there was no general agreement about how the Devil handed out his marks, neither was there any general agreement as to what a witch-mark looked like. Thus, although a suspected witch might have a suspicious-looking scar or lump on her skin, and her interrogators might strongly suspect that Satan had put it there, since countless other people, including the interrogators themselves, were likely to have similar marks, it was impossible to be absolutely sure.

It is in such situations that the skill and knowledge of a specialist becomes essential. Unfortunately, many of us are so gullible that often enough all someone has to do is declare himself an expert in a given field, and crowds of his fellow humans will enthusiastically accept him as such, even when hard evidence is conspicuously lacking. Thus it was that expert "searchers for the Devil's mark" came to the fore.

It was held that witch-marks were insensible to pain, and would not bleed if pierced. The easiest way of testing for witch-marks, therefore, was simply to stick a long pin into any likely-looking blemish, and this was the technique used by searchers for the mark in Scotland.

The most notorious of these charlatans was John Kincaid from Tranent, who made a living as a professional witch-pricker, travelling widely through southern Scotland in the practice of his trade, and apparently even venturing into England. He was called upon by ministers and kirk sessions, provosts and burgh councils, lairds and baron baillies, who had witchcraft suspects on their hands. The discovery of a "genuine" witch-mark by an acknowledged expert was not as absolutely incontrovertible guarantee of the suspect's guilt, but it provided very strong evidence for the prosecution.

Kincaid carried on a busy lucrative practice from the late 1640s until 1662, and although illiterate and far advanced in years, he seems to have been implicitly trusted, and treated almost like a licensed government official, being described time and time again as the "common" (i.e. public) searcher of witches. His first venture into pricking, according to his own testimony, had been when the minister of Tranent had asked him to prick marks on the body of a gardener's wife suspected of witchcraft. Presumably the minister was reluctant to soil his own hands with the job, and decided to delegate the

Tranent Parish Church: The minister of Tranent started John Kincaid on his career as a witch-pricker.

unpleasant task to someone less fastidious. Perhaps Kincaid was known to be particularly callous, or perhaps he was just standing by at the time. Whatever the reason, Kincaid seems to have pricked the suspect successfully, and realised that here was a way of making an easy living, and gaining not a little power and prestige into the bargain.

The basics of his trade were simple. He would search the suspect for likely marks, stripping her (or him) if necessary. When a mark was found Kincaid would run a long pin into it, right up to the head, if possible. If the mark did not bleed, and if the suspect felt no pain, he would certify the mark as diabolic in origin, and sign a statement to that effect with his initials "IK". The records contain many examples of Kincaid at work in East Lothian and nearby, and no doubt his activities will be documented far and wide across the country.

The Register of the Privy Council records Kincaid's presence in Dirleton in July 1649. Patrick Watson and his wife Manie Halyburton from West Fenton had been named as witches by Agnes Cockburn, a confessing witch in Dirleton who had been seduced into witchcraft by the Piper's Mother from Longniddry. According to Kincaid's own account, when Patrick and Manie heard that the witch pricker was in the vicinity, they voluntarily requested that he examine them for the Devil's mark – presumably because they were sure that he would find no such thing. On the contrary, however, Kincaid found a witch-mark a little below Patrick's left shoulder blade, and another on the left side of Manie Halyburton's neck. Kincaid testified, "They had no feeling in those marks, nor did any blood come from them after I had tested them in the same way as I had always done with others." This he did in the presence of a notary and several witnesses, including the Laird of Saltcoats and the baron baillie and chamberlain of Dirleton. Manie and Patrick were later tried, convicted, and executed in the usual way.

On receiving supplications from some suspects who had been imprisoned in Haddington for some time, but never brought to trial, Haddington Presbytery noted in September 1649 that they "had John Kincaid's testimony that these persons have the mark". In early October the Presbytery recommended to the magistrates of Haddington that Elspeth Dobie should be locked up and searched for the witches' mark. However, it transpired that John Kincaid, "the usual searcher for the witches' mark", was in England and would not return for another twenty days. Elspeth's sons asked that she should be released on bail, and Haddington Presbytery recommended to the baillies of the burgh that they should set bail at £1000 Scots, to be officially recorded in the town court books – a hefty sum, even if the pound Scots was worth only one twelfth of a pound sterling.

As we have already seen, Kincaid was present at the interrogation of Janet Bruce in Tranent. Among the records of the evidence gathered for her prosecution is a paper stating:

"Today, according to the orders of His Highness's justices of the peace in the western division of East Lothian, John Kincaid, witch investigator, searched and examined the body of Jonett Bruce now imprisoned in the prison house of Tranent. He found four marks, into which he inserted a pin of this length (59mm). This he did in four separate places in her body, without drawing blood, before the following witnesses: James Ainslie, son of Mr Cornelius Ainslie in Preston; Archibald Purvis and David Howieson, elders in the parish of Tranent; Alexander Mudy and James Cowan, constables there; Walter Scott, clerk to the justices of the said division. Also, John Kincaid declares that the four marks are of diabolical origin, and he will declare this upon oath, in confirmation of which he signs with his mark of two letters, at Tranent 30th June 1657.......................Signed: IK."

In the following year we find Kincaid in Dalkeith in Midlothian where he appeared on oath before the justices of the peace in the case of Catherine Casse as "witness to the mark, John Kincaid, pricker".

1659 saw Kincaid busy again in his home town of Tranent where a group of eleven witchcraft suspects had been rounded up. The evidence-gathering process and the trials themselves are well documented, particularly because two of the accused were acquitted, and after the Restoration of the monarchy the evidence was sifted through again to see if the acquittal under the previous regime could indeed be justified.

The suspects confessed to attending witch-meetings at the Brae Green between Seton and Tranent, and other meetings were mentioned at Preston Links, and the Heugh – a ravine just outside the village of Tranent. One of the suspects, Christian Cranston, seems to have been a healer in the traditional "wise wife" style, using foxglove leaves and south-running water, and asking God's blessing on her cures. John Douglas, the only man in the group, was a piper who, according to his confession, had been recruited by the Devil himself to play for dancing at local witch-meetings. The tune he played at the Brae Green was "Hulie, the bed will fall" ("Be careful, the bed will collapse" – the inference is fairly obvious!), and at Preston Links the witches danced to a spring called "Kilt thy coat Maggie, and go thy ways with me".

The documentation shows that as a result of Christian Cranston's confession she was searched for the "Devil's Mark". When she was examined by John Kincaid the "common searcher", he found the Devil's Mark under her left armpit, into which a "great long pin" was put. Another mark was also found on her leg. Both were insensible, and there was no blood at all. Since the pricking of witches has been portrayed by some writers as a kind of torture to force the suspect into a confession, it is interesting to read that in Christian's case it was the confession that led to the pricking, not the pricking that led to the confession!

John Douglas was found to have two witch-marks; one on the roof of his mouth, and another on his left leg. Janet Thomson met the Devil in the Heugh in the shape of a man in green clothes. After having sex with her, he put his hands round her neck where the marks were later found. Janet said that she supposed that was when she got the marks, although she had not been aware of getting them. When Marion Yool was examined by the "common searcher" in the presence of Thomas Kirkaldy, minister of Tranent, and three of his elders, he found a mark beneath her left armpit, with "a dug or teat of insensible flesh".

Barbara Cochrane's case is interesting. She submitted voluntarily to examination, saying that she would be happy to admit to being the Devil's servant if any mark was found on her, apart from the normal marks women were likely to have. Kincaid duly found two marks on the back or her neck, and pushed a "great long pin" into each of them, which Barbara apparently did not feel. When she realised what had happened, she cried out in the presence of the justices of the peace, "Foul thief, you have deceived me now! You have deceived me now!" and admitted that she was a witch. The Devil is often referred to as the Foul Thief, so did Barbara mean that the Devil had deceived her when she thought she was under his protection, or was the outburst directed at Kincaid who had pricked her painlessly, perhaps using some deceitful "trick of the trade"? It is, in fact, quite striking how often suspects seem to have given up protesting their innocence, admitting that they were indeed witches, as soon as witch-marks had been identified.

Out of this group of unfortunates, Marion Logan, Barbara Cochrane, John Douglas, Janet Crooks and Helen Simbeard were strangled and burnt in Tranent on 5th May; Marion Lyne and Christian Cranston were dispatched in the same place on 14th May, and Janet Man was executed on Edinburgh's Castle Hill on 11th May. Elspeth Fowler died in prison of dysentery, and Janet Thomson and Marion Yool were acquitted. As previously mentioned, Janet and Marion were re-investigated after the Restoration, but as there is no record of another trial, we must presume that their acquittal was sustained.

There was a flurry of witch trials in the early years of the Restoration, as the new brooms of the new regime strove to demonstrate their effectiveness, and we find a detailed account of Kincaid at work in Dalkeith – first of all on 18th June 1661 when he pricked Janet Cock. He found two marks on her, and pierced them "without the least appearance of blood. The holes stood open and unclosed, as if the pins had been put in white paper." Then on 11th July Kincaid examined Elspeth Graham: "In carrying out his duties he found a mark on her right side, and another below her left breast. He pricked these marks and put a pin into each of them, right up to the head, then pulled them out, without the appearance of any blood." The following day Katherine Hunter asked to be examined. She had not been accused of witchcraft, but requested Kincaid's services because of her "uneasy conscience". He found a mark on her left shoulder, and another in her left armpit. "He pricked them and left both the pins sticking in the marks without any sensation or feeling on her part until she put on her shirt again, after which she pulled them out with her own hand."

Also at work in Dalkeith in July 1661 was another witch pricker, John Ramsay from Ormiston. On 2nd August he was summoned to appear before the Privy Council to answer for pricking a certain Margaret Tait, who had died soon afterwards. Can this incident have given the Privy Council pause for thought regarding the whole business of witch pricking? Certainly, on 9th January 1662 the Council recommended that John Kincaid himself should be arrested, on the grounds that "he takes upon himself on his own authority without warrant or order to prick and investigate persons reputed to be guilty of the abominable crime of witchcraft". It was decided that Kincaid should be imprisoned until he found surety that he would appear before the Council to answer for his behaviour. On 31st March the Council noted that "great abuses" had been committed by Kincaid, and that as a result of his actions "in all probability many innocent people have suffered." The Council decided that Kincaid should be locked up in the Tolbooth of Edinburgh while investigations were made. This was duly done, and Kincaid was closely questioned about his methods. The paper recording his interrogation on 4th April is still in the Justiciary Court records. It shows that although Kincaid was now claiming that witch pricking was a simple business which could be done by anybody, he had not been above dressing up his "skills" to make them appear more impressive.

When asked how he acquired the skill of examining witches, he replied that he only did what he had learned "by sight", and what he had been told to do by witches themselves. Apparently he would not let suspects go over the threshold of the house where they were to be searched – presumably he had them carried in. He was in the habit of placing them an ell's distance from the wall. He claimed to have been told by witches that suspects should be taken into the house backwards, and kept away from the wall and from water. He always started his search for witch-marks by looking first at the suspect's hands and arms. He implied that no special skills were involved in pricking, saying that anyone who watched him do it would be able to do it himself.

Kincaid's questioner was obviously under the impression that Kincaid had told witchcraft suspects that he knew they had been with the Devil at a certain time in a certain place. Kincaid hotly denied this, however, saying that all he had said was that he could tell that the suspects were witches because of their unpleasant smell. He explained that he had been told by practising witches that in order to have sex with them, the Devil had to "put on" and inhabit the corpse of a dead man, the stink from which, not surprisingly, was left on his partners' bodies. (Whether or not there was any truth in this gruesome explanation, it certainly speaks volumes about the personal hygiene of the average witchcraft suspect!)

Kincaid was obviously at pains to convince his questioners that his skills were quite ordinary, and that anything resembling a ritual was only done because witches themselves had said it would be helpful. It sounds rather as if there was a suspicion that Kincaid himself might have acquired "unlawful" powers. This may have been because a vagabond boy, James Welsh, had been swept up in the East Lothian witch hunt of

1661, claiming to have attended many witch meetings, and naming droves of local people as witches. Significantly, he claimed to have been at a meeting at "Tranent Moor Cross" where he saw the Devil and John Kincaid sitting side by side. Welsh was eventually more or less dismissed as a time-waster and let off with a year and a day in Edinburgh's "Correction House", but his statement may well have led the authorities to ponder whether there might be something of the supernatural in Kincaid's ability to identify witches. Was his skill the gift of Satan? Could he identify witches because he was one himself? Any supporting evidence could of course have led to Kincaid suffering the same fate to which he had cheerfully consigned so many others.

Well over a month after his interrogation Kincaid was still languishing in the Tolbooth. He petitioned the Privy Council for release, claiming to be so ill and infirm that his life was in danger. He asked to be released on condition that he would return to prison if required, and on condition that he would not prick witchcraft suspects without permission from the Council. The Privy Council was in no hurry to oblige, however, and on 12th June Kincaid appealed again, saying that he was an old man, infirm and ill, and once more guaranteeing not to prick without a warrant from the Council, and promising to find caution that he would return to custody if called upon. The Council then decided to allow the Edinburgh magistrates to release him under these conditions, adding that if he pricked any witchcraft suspect in future without a warrant from a judge or from the Council, he would be answerable "at his utmost peril". On the following day, June 13th, John Somervale, skinner, burgess of Edinburgh, registered as cautioner for Kincaid's good behaviour, and with that, John Kincaid, Scotland's most notorious witch-pricker, disappears from the records, presumably to spend his twilight years in Tranent in decent obscurity.

The Peaston Witches

On 20th September 1628 four convicted witches were burned on Peaston Moor, south of Ormiston. These would appear to be the last confirmed executions for witchcraft in East Lothian. They were the result of a localised witchcraft panic in certain parts of East and Midlothian, which began when two Prestonpans women, Agnes Kelly and her servant Marjory Anderson, were arrested and confessed to witchcraft, and the Privy Council granted an application to have them tried by commission. The eminent judge Lord Fountainhall, whose voluminous "Historical Notices" record all the interesting and unusual events which drew his attention, explains how the first two suspects named others who in turn denounced many more from the parishes of Humbie, Keith, Ormiston and Pencaitland in East Lothian, and in Crichton, Fala and Loanhead in Midlothian. The disgraced minister of Crichton, Gideon Penman, who had been dismissed for sexual indiscretions, was also named as one who danced with the witches, and was referred to by the Devil as "Mr Gideon, my chaplain". Not only that, but the confessing witches "were ready to condemn by their accusations several gentlewomen and others of fashion". This, however, was a step too far, and it was decided to pay no heed to these slanderous accusations, which could only be the product of delusion or malice, it being impossible that such persons could have been present at anything as low and uncouth as witch meetings.

Marion Veitch from Keith confessed on 21st June 1678 before the laird, minister, and schoolmaster of Keith, and several others, that she had first entered the Devil's service many years before, around 1650, at a place called the Red Ford. She had placed one hand on her head and the other on the sole of her foot, and delivered up to the Devil all between her two hands. She renounced her baptism, and had sex with the Devil – the first of several such frolics - and attended a witch meeting in Ormiston Wood where many people were present, and all danced with the Devil. She claimed to have been present, but invisible, when Helen Laing killed her own husband on his death bed by pulling out his heart. A week later, Marion confirmed her involvement in the death of Helen Laing's husband, and admitted that she had also been involved in the killing of a young girl in Templehall.

On 1st July, in the presence of several witnesses including the Laird of Keith, and the schoolmaster of Peaston, Margaret Dodds from Peaston made a "free and voluntary" confession which was taken down by William Cockburn, schoolmaster of Keith. She said the Devil had appeared to her while she was in bed at home three years previously. She had renounced her baptism, and at the Devil's request put one hand on her head, the other on her knee, and gave over everything between her two hands. The usual practice was of course to put one hand on the crown of the head and the other on the sole of a foot, but Margaret was not able to reach the sole of her foot, presumably because she was too old and arthritic to do so. She was not, however, to old and arthritic to have sex with the Devil. She testified that his penis was cold, and he did not seem to be breathing – which rather seems to tie in with John Kincaid's notion of the Devil inhabiting a dead man's corpse in order to have sex. The cold penis is par for the course in witchcraft confessions, but the want of breath is more unusual. Margaret admitted to having subsequently attending a witch meeting at Murrays Burn where the company danced to the music of a piper. Surprisingly, the Devil was not present, but Margaret named several women who were. She herself, she claimed, was not able to dance.

Isobel Eliot had been denounced as a witch by Marion Veitch, and Marion Campbell from Peaston. Isobel was from

Peaston : Four witches were hanged and burnt near here in 1678 – possibly East Lothian's last witch burnings.

Templehall in Pencaitland parish, and made her confession before the ministers of Pencaitland and Humbie, among others. She claimed that two years previously, when she was employed as a servant to Helen Laing in Peaston, her mistress prevented her from going to church one Sunday morning, saying she was expecting a visit from a friend. Coming into the house with water from the well, Isobel found her mistress Helen Laing with Marion Campbell, and the Devil sitting between them. When the other two women left the room, the Devil kissed Isobel, and suggested having sex. Isobel refused him, saying she was pregnant, and the Devil promised to leave her alone until after her child was born. She renounced her baptism at the Devil's request, and he waved his hand before her face. She felt what seemed like a sprinkling of dew, with which he "baptised" her, giving her the new name of "Jean". After the birth of her child she had sex with the Devil – the first of several occasions. His body was very cold, she said, and he lay on her with the weight of four men.

Isobel named several other women as witches, including two women in Loanhead whom she accused of killing one of the Lasswade minister's children, and the daughter of a coalminer there. She also confessed to having been present with other witches when they contrived the death of William Hair's daughter, but denied being involved in the death of Helen Laing's husband.

Unusually, Isobel described a meeting where there was a blazing fire, and the Devil gave those present a form of Communion, then preached a blasphemous sermon. It must be said that this is most unusual for East Lothian, where any form of "religious" ritual is almost completely absent from the records, apart from Satan's famous appearance in the pulpit at the great witch meeting at North Berwick.

Isobel also said that she had been present when William Thomson's child was poisoned by Marion Veitch, the child's own grandmother. She declared that she and Marion Veitch had been in the shape of bumble bees at the time, and that Marion had carried the poison to her grandchild in her claws, wings, and mouth. On another occasion Isobel had left her own body sitting in Pencaitland church while she travelled to Loanhead in the shape of a crow to see a child she had nursed there.

Helen Laing from Peaston made her confession there on 29th June. The records state that it was a "free and voluntary" confession, made "without any torture or threatening" before her minister Mr Sinclair of Ormiston, among others, and taken down by William Cockburn, schoolmaster of Keith. According to Helen, the Devil had first appeared to her seven years ago in her own garden at Peaston. A year later, she met him again at a witch meeting at the Ward Burn. Again, he appeared as a black man in black clothes, and this time she renounced her baptism at his request. She remembered another meeting at the Black Saugh, but the only people she recognised at these meetings were Marion Campbell and Margaret Dodds.

Helen denied ever causing harm to her husband William Laing, denied ever doing any harm to anyone, and indeed denied knowing anyone else who ever did any such thing. She also denied ever having sex with the Devil.

Many other women were rounded up and questioned, most describing the same initiation ritual of laying one hand on the crown of the head, the other on the sole of a foot, and giving over to the Devil everything in between. Several of them admitted receiving new names from the Devil. Many meetings are mentioned, but only Helen Laing mentioned a diabolical sacrament. Several women who were called in for questioning simply disappeared rather than face the ordeal, and were "put to the horn" or outlawed. Probably Northumberland would be the safest place to lie low, since it is unlikely that England would have extradited witchcraft suspects at that late date.

One intriguing figure, mentioned again and again in the course of interrogations, is Sara Cranstoun. From statements given by various witnesses, we can work out that Sara was the widow of George Anderson. She lived in Nether Keith in a house that was large enough to contain a "hall" with a fireplace. She had a son John Anderson who was well enough off to own a horse, and she had a daughter who was "Laird Skirvin's lady". Sara also had a servant Jennet Burton, who according to one report, used to carry Sara's mantle for her to witch meetings. All this suggests someone from a relatively prosperous background; perhaps from a substantial farming family, able to hob-nob with and marry into the lower echelons of the landowning classes. Sara was reported to have been present at several witch meetings, sometimes arriving on her son's horse, which she apparently eventually "burst" and rode to death. According to Isobel Eliot, she was also present at the contriving of the death of William Hair's daughter. Anna Dalgleish described being in Sara's house at two o' clock in the afternoon when there was no-one else there but Sara. A black man appeared, and Sara took Anna's hand. The dusky guest was of course the Devil. He kissed Anna and they had sex. She then renounced her baptism, and putting one hand on her head and the other on the sole of her foot, she gave over all between her hands to the Devil. On another occasion Sara roused Anna out of her bed at midnight and brought her out to where the Devil was waiting for her by Sara's front door.

Bessie Gourlay, a midwife from Fala, said it was Sara who had seduced her into serving the Devil. Bessie must have been pregnant at the time, for Sara said that if Bessie would promise to do her bidding, she would get her daughter, "Laird Skirvin's lady", to attend her in childbirth. Sara took Bessie into her garden to meet a gentleman, and said that if she would agree to serve that gentleman, she would never want. Sara explained that this was a gentleman who had come from her daughter at Ladyside, and Bessie politely asked after the health of the family there. Later, she realised that the "gentleman" had been the Devil. On another occasion Bessie went out to her barn and found Sara there. Sara beckoned her to follow, and took her up to "the Whithouse" where the Devil was waiting. There Bessie renounced her baptism, and with one hand on her head and the other on her foot, gave herself over to the Devil. Bessie also mentioned as a bitter afterthought that Sara had promised to give her a cheese, but never did so.

Sara's servant Jennet Burton declared that two years previously her mistress had got her out of bed saying she must come and speak to a gentleman. Sara brought her out into the hall, where a grim black man was waiting. He took her in his arms and kissed her, and the following evening had sex with her by the fireplace in the hall. A fortnight later Sara took her to a witch meeting where she renounced her baptism, and with one hand on her head and the other on the sole of her foot, gave all in between to the Devil. He then gave her a new name, calling her "Sara's Drudge".

At the last meeting before the round-up of suspects began, according to Bessie Gourlay, Sara was present, masked and wrapped up in a cloak. Sara declared, "The witches will be arrested now, but I won't confess. I've been in his service a long time, but now I'm going to give it up."

It would seem from the plentiful evidence given against her that not only was Sara Cranstoun constantly involved in witchcraft shenanigans in the district, but would appear to have been something of a leading light. It seems quite incredible, therefore, that there is no record of her even having been questioned. Lord Fountainhall, as we have seen, wrote that the authorities intervened when it seemed that the suspects were about to name "gentlewomen and others of fashion". We can only assume that if Sara was not actually a "gentlewoman" herself, she must have been sufficiently well connected to the gentry to ensure her safety. Neither did "Sara's Drudge" Jennet Burton face trial, although she had confessed to the Diabolic Pact.

Others were not so lucky. Bessie Gourlay, Agnes Somervaill, and Margaret Sonnes were sentenced to be strangled and burnt at the Gallowlee between Edinburgh and Leith; and Margaret Douglas, Margaret Low, Margaret Small, Isobel Eliot, Marion Veitch, Helen Laing, Margaret Dodds, Isobel Shanks and Helen Forester were also condemned to death. Douglas, Low, Shanks, and Forester were burned in Edinburgh, and the remaining four sentenced to die on Peaston Moor on 20th September between the hours of two and four in the afternoon.

Although the sentence pronounced on Isobel Eliot, Marion Veitch, Helen Laing, and Margaret Dodds says quite specifically that they were to be strangled to death at a stake and their bodies thereafter burned to ashes, it seems that in fact they were hanged. The register of the Privy Council contains the record of the expenses incurred in carrying out the sentence of the court, and it is noted that the sum of £1-10-0 was paid "to the wright and his men for building the gallows and the scaffold", and that £2-5-6 was paid "for wood and nails for building the gallows and scaffold". Perhaps by 1678 it was felt that garrotting at the stake was a little primitive and old fashioned. It also raises the possibility that other victims of "the stake" in previous years in East Lothian and elsewhere might also have been hanged.

The records give an intriguing hint at kind of local government cock-up which would not seem out of place in our own times. The payment recorded to the Haddington hangman is for his wages, his expenses incurred before he came out to Peaston, and also "for sending him back with a merk to buy ropes". We picture the hangman arriving, keen to get on with the job, and asking, "Right, where are the ropes?"

"The ropes? Did you not bring the ropes?"

"It's not my job to bring the ropes. You're supposed to supply them."

"No, we just assumed you'd bring them. How do you expect to hang somebody without ropes?"

"Exactly! It's my job to hang the criminals, not to supply ropes."

And so the hangman was sent back to Haddington for the crucial equipment. We can only hope that this little administrative hiccup took place well before the appointed hour for execution and that the wretched victims were not kept waiting by the scaffold while their executioner made his way to the county town and back.

The final part of the sentence was carried out with "8 cart loads of coal at 14 shillings per cart", and four tar barrels costing £2-9-4.

The authorities must have been keen to ensure that the sentence was carried out satisfactorily and with propriety, for several local lairds and ministers were required to sign and send in a certificate to that effect to the Privy Council. At that late date in the 16th century, there might also have been an element of the Privy Council ensuring that the local dignitaries out in the sticks were made thoroughly aware of the full horror of the consequences to the victims of the accusations, the interrogations, and the sentence of the court. The certificate reads, "We, the undersigned testify that we were all present, saw, and were eyewitnesses to the execution of the foresaid sentence of death upon the bodies of the four witches above named, at the time, day, and place above mentioned. This conformed to the foresaid sentence of death in all particulars.

In witness of this, and of the truth of these particulars, we the forenamed persons have signed this with our hands at Peaston Moor, 20th September 1678.

William Baillie of Lamington

Adam Cockburn of Ormiston

William Cunynghame of Eterkine, younger

David Hepburn of Randerstoun (?)

Mr Robert and Mr George Cockburns, uncles to the Laird of Ormiston

William Borthwick of Johnstonburn

John Belshes of that Ilk

Mr John Sinclair, minister at Ormiston

Mr James Calderwood, minister at Humbie

Mr Robert Spottswood, minister at Crichton

Mr James Cockburn, minister at Pencaitland

Mr George Moodie, minister at Fala

Mr George Grierson, reader at Ormiston."

The deaths of Isobel Eliot, Marion Veitch, and Helen Laing are the last authenticated witch burnings in East Lothian. There may, however, have been one other.

Dunbar Tolbooth: Catherine McTarget stood trial here for witchcraft in 1688 – East Lothian's last witchcraft trial.

Catherine McTarget

East Lothian's last witchcraft trial was held in the Tolbooth of Dunbar on 30th May 1688, under the terms of a commission from the Privy Council. The Council had stipulated in advance, that before sentence was passed, the verdict of the jury and the records of the trial were to be sent in so that the Commissioners might be given "further direction". In those latter years of the 17th century the Privy Council was seemingly keeping a close eye on witchcraft trials, which were becoming something of a rarity.

The accused was Catherine McTarget, wife of William Broun, weaver and burgess of Dunbar. She had long been a well-known character in the area, an object of fear to some, and a public nuisance in the eyes of others. There had been previous attempts at prosecution. She is listed in 1678 as fugitive from a charge of witchcraft, and the burgh records of Dunbar state that in 1683 she had failed to appear in court on another charge of witchcraft. Orders were given to John Laidlaw the public executioner to put her out of the burgh, beyond its bounds. Finally, however, she had been locked up in the Tolbooth and closely questioned, while lengthy statements were taken down in evidence against her from the legions of those who had got on her wrong side.

Just how much of a menace Catherine was perceived to be, is indicated by the length of her "dittay" or indictment, which contains twenty five items, if we exclude the final two which refer merely to her supposed confession in the Tolbooth. The earliest charge refers to an incident in 1658, and the latest to the year of her trial, 1688. It is obvious that Catherine was eccentric in the extreme, if not actually mentally ill. She had quite deliberately chosen to stravaig around the countryside as a beggar, although as the preamble to her dittay emphasises, there was absolutely no necessity to do so, for her husband the weaver had a perfectly adequate income. Catherine seems to have actively taken pleasure in spreading fear and unease among the local population, not only by making the kind of vague threats and enigmatic statements typical of witchcraft suspects, but by peremptorily demanding alms, imperiously insisting on more if not satisfied, and threatening misfortune and disaster if she was refused. Her dittay notes that far from being ashamed or indignant that she was believed to be a witch, she actually gloried in her reputation. This hardly seems an exaggeration, for it is clear from several of the items in her indictment that Catherine gave every indication of deriving enjoyment from terrifying people out of heir wits. At times she seems to be going out of her way to act the part of the malevolent witch, and it is difficult to avoid the conclusion that she had no-one to blame but herself for her indictment for witchcraft.

Several of the charges in Catherine's indictment refer to threats she made, either vague or specific, which apparently resulted in misfortune or even death. The first of these dates from 1658. In that year Catherine had quarrelled with John Milne because his horse got into her vegetable garden and trampled some of her plants. Catherine predicted that before the horse got home again it would break its neck, and that very night the horse fell over the cliffs and broke its neck as Catherine had foretold. As for John Milne, Catherine predicted that he would never thrive, and although he was a sober man of substantial means, his wealth and possessions subsequently melted away, until he fell into abject poverty.

In 1672, Catherine's husband William Broun decided to sell a cow of theirs to James Reid, a Dunbar butcher. This infuriated Catherine, and when the deal was being discussed she shouted up the stair to her husband that if Reid bought the cow he would never draw blood from her. Within a day or two Reid fell ill and died after a short illness, although he had been in perfect health up until then.

Two years later Catherine spoke to Andrew Stevenson as he was sowing oats at Bourhouses, and asked him for a boll of oats. This was presumably meant as a joke or sarcastic banter, for a boll was a large quantity of grain, over 200 litres dry measure, and in any case the seed was not Stevenson's to give, for he was not the farmer, only a farm servant. Stevenson replied that it was a boll of coals Catherine deserved, to burn her with. Catherine then went up to his house to ask for a drink of water. Stevenson admitted when questioned that when he came in he had struck Catherine because she would not get up and go away. A day or two later Stevenson's wife encountered Catherine at the mill, and after speaking to her, came home and "ramished to death" – went raving mad and died.

John Fergusson was loading coal on Dunbar shore in 1677, when Catherine attempted to steal some coal out of his cart. Fergusson was incensed, and struck her. Catherine told him the coal would be dear coal to him – in other words he would pay a heavy price for it – and he would never strike another blow. Fergusson, a healthy young man, went home, fell ill, and never came out of his house again alive. According to a witness, he took a "languishing disease" and "sweated to death".

In the same year of 1677, Catherine came begging to the Knowes, and asked for alms at George Shirreff's house. His wife Christian Orme had been making porridge, and she offered Catherine the porridge pot to lick. Catherine asked for some milk or ale with it, then when Christian obliged by giving her some weak ale, complained that it was tasteless and said there was better in the house. Christian said that there was, but said it was a brew that had not yet had yeast put in it to ferment it. Catherine said it would ferment enough before long, and she had no sooner left the house than the unfermented brew foamed up out of the barrel with such violence that it splashed the beams of the ceiling. The servants came running with buckets to catch as much as they could, and the entire household was bewildered, and not a little frightened, as the brew had never had a drop of yeast added to it.

On Handsel Monday of 1682, the New Year holiday, Patrick Fergusson was watching a quoits match, when Catherine offered him some bread and cheese, which he refused. She pressed him, and he took a bite or two, then handed it back. Catherine let it drop to the ground, and that very day Fergusson's wife fell ill and died less than a fortnight later.

Catherine came begging to James Lauder's house one day in the same year, and got a handful of meal from Lauder's wife Katherine Sandilands. Not content with the oatmeal, Catherine asked for a drink of ale as well. Lauder's wife refused to give her any, but Catherine stood where she was and refused to move, and eventually the woman was forced to give her a drink to get rid of her. As soon as Catherine was gone, Lauder's wife took a violent pain in her hand. She was bled by a Dr McCullo who happened to be in the house, but the pain would not go away, and the doctor expressed the opinion that she was being afflicted by some evil person. Soon afterwards, Catherine McTarget arrived back at the house. Lauder's wife shouted, "Away with you!" and Catherine replied, "God help you, you'll never be well till either you or your child die!" Lauder's wife's child was a young baby at the breast. It died within a few days, and the pain in the dead infant's mother's hand grew less every day from then on until it disappeared completely.

Catherine came begging in 1684 to the house of Thomas Ross, a blacksmith in East Barns. His daughter was making porridge, and Catherine asked for some. The girl replied that she would rather see her choke on it. Catherine retorted that some of her own family would choke before long, and that very night the girl's father Thomas Ross choked on a piece of beef in a neighbour's house, and died.

On Handsel Monday of the year of her trial, 1688, Catherine came seeking alms at the house of Thomas Whyte, cooper in Dunbar, and his wife gave her something. Catherine became aware that Thomas Whyte's brother John from the Cove was in the house, and had sent out for a pint of ale (a Scots pint, by the way, was around 1.7 litres) and so she came back later asking for some of it. John Whyte called her a witch, and said he'd see her hanged and burnt before she got any of it, and Catherine snapped back that she wished there might be a hanged man about John's house before too long. A couple of months later, John Whyte's next door neighbour in the Cove hanged himself, and his corpse was carried out past John's door.

It was expected of witches that they would have foreknowledge of mishaps, even if they were not themselves the author of the misfortune, and Catherine displayed his ability twice in the year 1684. On the first occasion she arrived at a house on the West Links of Dunbar, and hearing a young calf bawling loudly, she asked what was wrong with it. The goodwife of the house explained that it was needing its dinner. "Hout," said Catherine, "it was calved at an ebb tide. It will roar till it dies." And indeed, the calf continued to bawl "in an extraordinary manner" until it died a few days later.

In the same year a Dunbar seaman, William Henderson, made his way down to the shore accompanied by his wife, to join his ship. As they were saying goodbye to each other, Catherine McTarget was heard to remark, "You may take leave of each other, for it will be a long goodnight." Within a few days the ship was wrecked and William Henderson was drowned. One witness remarked that Henderson's wife could never again look at Catherine after the loss of her husband.

There were other activities and behaviours deemed to be typical of witches, and not surprisingly these also turn up on Catherine's charge-sheet. One of the most common acts of malefice attributed to Scottish witches was causing cows to give blood instead of milk. In 1683 Catherine came begging to James Forrester's door and asked for milk. His wife retorted, "You'll get no milk here!" The next time the Forresters' cow was milked, it produced only blood. This continued for two of three days, and then the cow died.

Another incident involved throwing down a horsehair tether, something "usually done by witches", according to Item 6 in Catherine's dittay. In the Highlands, the cow-fetter used to prevent cows from walking off when being milked, was believed to be used by witches to cause impotence in men, but in Catherine's case she was accused of having used the tether to cause illness and death. Catherine had come to John Lawrie's house on a Sunday morning. She was seen first to throw down a hair tether, and then to peer into the room where Lawrie was lying sleeping. Lawrie looked up and saw her, and was immediately overwhelmed by "a most unnatural disease", and never closed his eyes again until he died on the morning of the following Thursday. A neighbour described how Lawrie had to be tied down on his bed, for he was snapping and biting at everything around him, in "an extraordinary distemper", and crying out, "There she is! There she is!" Both the neighbour and Lawrie's wife had noticed that on the morning of Catherine's visit there was an unusually large number of crows flying around the house and making a tremendous noise.

We have already seen how the East Barns witch Isobel Young was in the habit of throwing down her head-cloths to cause misfortune or to intimidate the gullible. Events took a similar turn when Catherine fell out with Janet Symontone. Janet asked Catherine for a peck of barley, and Catherine for some reason became enraged. Janet in turn called Catherine "an incarnate devil", whereupon Catherine snatched off her head-cloths and threw them at Janet. Janet had a batch of good malt steeping, from which she had been brewing good ale, but after her quarrel with Catherine, neither Janet nor anyone else could manage to brew ale from the malt, which had become utterly useless.

It was expected of witches that they would be able to cure sickness and disease. This, of course, is typically a "wise wife" activity, and it is perhaps significant that there is not much evidence of this sort of thing in Catherine McTarget's dittay. It underlines her status as public nuisance rather than healer – or in modern parlance, as a "black witch" rather than a "white witch". There is one example of Catherine taking the role of a healer, however.

Catherine had wanted to buy a sheep's head from the wife of William McKie, a Dunbar butcher; but another woman, Jean Johnston, offered more money for it and was given the head, prompting Catherine to remark that the head would do her family no good. As she was boiling the sheep's head Jean began to feel ill, and suffered in agony for several days. Hearing gossip that she was responsible for bewitching Jean, Catherine came to her house with some onions, and gave instructions to boil up three of them with some sheep's entrails. As soon as Jean tasted the broth she became well again, and testified later on oath to the truth of the cure and her recovery.

Since witchcraft was punishable by death, it might be expected that practising witches would try to keep a low profile. Catherine, on the contrary, seems to have gone out of her way to exhibit eccentric and menacing behaviour. For example, she was seen riding a white-faced calf down Dunbar High Street in the dark, at ten o' clock at night. When she was asked what she was up to, Catherine replied that the calf belonged to Margaret Siddel; she had found it at the kirk style, and was taking it home. Riding it down the High Street, needless to say, was not the way that the normal douce indweller of Dunbar would have chosen to return it to its owner.

The year before Catherine's trial, two girls, one aged seven and the other eleven, were walking out of Dunbar near Catherine's house. To their surprise, they found Catherine lying in the middle of the main road, in a very strange posture. Suddenly, she shot out her head and her feet, leaped up, and chased the terrified girls down the road. When they reached home, according to their father, both fell sick, and the younger girl found herself struck dumb. The next day, incredibly, Catherine arrived at their door asking for milk.

The girls' father, Patrick Wood, drew a knife, and swore to Catherine that he would be the death of her if she did not make his daughter speak again. Catherine prudently collapsed at Wood's feet, his wife dragged her enraged husband away, and Catherine quickly hurried off. Immediately, the younger daughter recovered her power of speech, and both girls became well from that moment on.

James Congalton owed Catherine money for some plants, and she came looking for it a month before it was due. Not surprisingly, Congalton was not keen to oblige. Nevertheless, Catherine would not take no for an answer, and refused to leave the vicinity of his house. She sat all night on a neighbouring stair, with her hair hanging over her eyes, presumably glowering at Congalton's house all the while. He was so terrified that he paid her the following day. All the same, it was said that he never did well after that, and became so poor that he was unable even to provide oatmeal for his children.

Very early one Sunday, around three or four o' clock in the morning, Catherine was seen bringing a bullock down the street in Dunbar. She left it outside William Bryson's byre, picked up some dung from the midden, and held it to the bullock's mouth, muttering "some words and charms". From then on, the cow which had been standing in Bryson's byre began to decline in health, and was never the same again.

It is quite clear that Catherine's reputation was so formidable that her very presence was enough to put some people in a state of alarm. When she came to George Colm's house in Spott begging at the door, Colm's teenage daughter and the servant maid were so frightened that they prayed God's blessing on themselves. Catherine remarked that they hadn't been so keen on praying before the saw her pleasant face, and staring at them fixedly, she pointedly asked the "Evil Spirit" to take note of the girls. Then she dipped her fingers in the water pail, touched them to the sole of her foot, and left. Shortly afterwards, three of George Colm's cows, and two of his bullocks died.

Such notoriety of course meant that perfectly innocent or meaningless actions could be interpreted in the worst possible light. The year before her trial, Catherine came to Patrick Mathie's house in Dunbar, sat down, and asked for milk. She then repeated three times, "If I break my nose, I spoil my face, and when I spoil my face I break my fortune." What she meant by this, if indeed she meant anything, is a mystery, but it was certainly deemed to be significant. Mathie gave her some milk, which did not please his daughter, who seems to have been the lady of the house. The following Sunday Catherine appeared at Mathie's door again with some cloth which she wanted to pawn for money. Mathie's daughter was scandalised that Catherine should appear on such an errand on the Sabbath, and sent her packing with a flea in her ear. This incident seems to have affected Mathie's daughter's mental equilibrium, for ever since she had remained sunk in a "melancholy and troubled" frame of mind.

George Fergusson, a little boy four years old, was playing in the street in Dunbar, throwing his bonnet around. Catherine picked it up, and placed it on his head upside down. This, it was reported, had been "by way of a charm". When the child came home he told his father his head was hurting. He then cried "most piteously" for three or four days, and died.

One action which must have been noted as carrying great significance was not carried out by Catherine, but performed on her by someone else. In 1683 Catherine was among a crowd on Dunbar shore at the time of the fishing – probably the seasonal herring "drave". A dumb man came up behind her and ran a long pin into her shoulder. She gave no sign of having noticed it, and when he took it out and held it up in front of several onlookers, Catherine reviled him for a "dumb devil" and walked away.

Two charges in Catherine's indictment seem to have made a particular impression, no doubt because both involved substantial numbers of witnesses. The first of these, Article 20 in the indictment, took place at the Knowes, four years before the misadventure with the exploding ale at the same place. Catherine had come to Patrick Shirreff's house at the Knowes selling onions. Shirreff's wife Helen Pringle had apparently allowed Catherine to sleep in a barn where pease straw was stored, but she was reluctant to buy any of the onions. Helen was heavily pregnant, and when her labour pains came on, Catherine was put out of her lodgings, possibly on the grounds that it was not wise to have such an inauspicious character around at such an important time. Catherine then visited Helen's neighbour Christian Orme, George Shirreff's wife. Christian was lying desperately ill, apparently on the point of death, but Catherine told her to cheer up, for what had been intended for her was going to land on another, and within four days Christian would be as well as she had ever been. Within four days, as predicted, Christian had made a seemingly miraculous recovery, and was able not only to get out of bed, but went to visit her neighbours, which caused much astonishment. Four days after being brought to childbed, however, Helen Pringle fell ill, and suffered in great pain for six months before recovering. The talk of the surrounding countryside was that Helen had been wronged by Catherine's witchcraft, for it was obvious to everyone that Christian Orme's sickness had been lifted from her and laid on Helen Pringle. When interviewed before Catherine's trial, Helen Pringle added that when some of the pea-chaff, from the barn where Catherine had slept, was fed to the horses, her husband's two best horses died within a fortnight. On the other hand, Christian Orme's husband George Shirreff, "farmer in the Knowes", said he knew nothing of the contents of Article 20 except by hearsay, and had nothing further to add. Such healthy scepticism, fortunately, would soon become the norm in Lowland Scotland.

Article 19 of Catherine's dittay related how she had come to the Post House at Cockburnspath and asked a servant there for a drink. The servant girl, Helen Paterson, refused, and Catherine went away muttering. Almost immediately, Helen fell to the ground senseless, and was carried to bed where she lay delirious for several hours. When John Home the postmaster was informed of what was going on, he instructed a manservant to go and find Catherine, and bring her back. The servant, John Ker, caught up with Catherine at Birnieknowes and persuaded her to return. When she arrived at the Post House she found Helen delirious in bed with several people holding her down. Catherine remarked that the girl had not been "well sained" that day (protected from evil by prayer or ritual), but that she would be fine if she was given a drink. She ordered an egg to be mixed up with ale, and administered the concoction to Helen with her own hand. Helen testified that when she had tasted a little of it she soon recovered. John Home the postmaster, indeed, stated that Helen got up "immediately", and got on with her work.

While she was imprisoned in the Tolbooth of Dunbar, Catherine admitted to the parish minister Thomas Wood that she was a witch, and that she had been taught by a Highland woman named Margaret McClain. She further admitted, reluctantly, that when Margaret McClain had told her to renounce her baptism, she had done so. The minister asked her if she would abide by this confession, and Catherine answered, "I will, for God knows everything." Nevertheless, it was not much of a confession. There was no mention of sexual or social intercourse with Satan, no mention of witch meetings, and apparently no admission of the truth of the individual accusations in her indictment. When questioned about some of these, Catherine gave evasive answers, made excuses, or claimed to have been only joking.

On 30th May Catherine was found guilty of the crimes of "witchcraft, sorcery, and superstition" by a jury of fifteen, all of whom were from Dunbar and the surrounding area, and all of whom would either be well acquainted with Catherine, or well aware of her reputation. The verdict of the trial was sent in, as required, to the Privy Council which, as previously mentioned, had stipulated that the court should not pronounce sentence until the Council had perused the records of the case. In his "Historical Notices", the 17th Century legal luminary Sir John Lauder of Fountainhall relates how the Privy Council was very sceptical about Catherine's guilt, and called her in to Edinburgh for questioning twice after her trial. Apparently she had been found guilty by a majority of only two. In the end, however, the Privy Council sent her back to Dunbar "to be burnt there if her judges pleased."

Perhaps significantly, Fountainhall does not seem to know whether she was in fact put to death or not. Surely, if a death sentence for witchcraft had been carried out – an unusual event by 1688 – Fountainhall would have been aware of it. Certainly, there seems to be no mention in the Dunbar records, or anywhere else, of Catherine McTarget's execution, so perhaps the Commissioners decided to be merciful. Thus, although Catherine was East Lothian's last convicted witch, it is just possible that she was spared the dubious honour of being the victim of East Lothian's last witch burning.

Marion Lillie

A Stone at the roadside just to the west of the village of Spott has been known traditionally as "The Witches' Stone". In recent years the immediate surroundings have been tidied up, and a plaque provided which states among other things that Marion Lillie was burnt here for witchcraft. The plaque is only repeating what has been claimed by several local historians, and not a few writers on witchcraft, but it is almost certainly wrong. All the evidence points to the conclusion that not only was Marion not burnt at the Witches' Stone, but that she was not burnt anywhere, and indeed was never even put on trial for witchcraft. The Witches' Stone in all likelihood does mark the spot where a witch or witches were put to death, but the association of Marion Lillie with the stone arises from local historians jumping to conclusions based on misleading statements made by the writer of the entry for Spott parish in the Old Statistical Account.

The parish minister, the Rev. John Martin, wrote in his account of Spott, "The records of the session are still extant, as far back as the 2d November 1662. The following particulars are extracted from them, with a view to explaining the general nature of these records, and as they tend to throw more light on the ancient state of the country." Among the passages purportedly quoted from the Kirk Session minutes are the following :

"1698 The session after a long examination of witnesses, refer the case of Marion Lillie for imprecation and supposed witchcraft, to the presbytery, who refer her for trial to the civil magistrate – said Marion generally called the 'Rigwoody Witch'."

The Witches' Stone, Spott: "Offerings" of flowers and coins are regularly left on the stone nowadays.

"Oct 1705 Many witches burnt on the top of Spott Loan."

These passages are given in quotation marks in John Martin's account, as if they were being quoted verbatim from the Kirk Session minutes; but the first is in fact the writer's own short summary of the Marion Lillie affair, and the second is probably a brief note he made regarding something he had been told.

Let us deal first of all with the statement that many witches were burnt at the top of Spott Loan in 1705. The Kirk Session minutes for the period 1704-1727 are exceptionally neat and legible, and there is no mention whatever in October 1705, or anywhere else in that volume, of witches being burnt. Nor is there any such mention in the preceding volume (1683-1703). Occasionally parish clerks would make brief notes of important events in other parish records, but there is no such note concerning witch burnings in the church's financial account books, nor in the records of baptisms, burials, and marriages. In any case, 1705 is very late for witch burnings. The last Scottish execution for witchcraft supposedly took place in Dornoch in 1727 (although there seems to be no authentic contemporary written evidence for it), but by the end of the 17th century the Privy Council had ceased granting permission for trials by commission, and the High Court of Justiciary was regularly dismissing witchcraft cases. Thus, the possibility of "many witches" being burnt in Spott in 1705 is remote in the extreme. The victims would have had to be put on trial, and there is no trace of any such trials in the records of the Privy Council or of the High Court of Justiciary, the only bodies competent to conduct or give permission for witchcraft trials. Perhaps Mr Martin was thinking of the six witchcraft suspects from Spott who were tried by commission in 1661. Since they had all confessed, they would most probably be found guilty and executed, quite possibly at the top of Spott Loan. Mr Martin might have jotted down a note on these executions and later copied the wrong date. Or had he somewhere seen a reference to witch burnings in 1605?

Whatever the explanation, it bears repetition that there is no mention in the Spott Kirk Session minutes of witch burnings in 1705, and the Old Statistical Account is simply wrong to say that there is.

As for "The Rigwoody Witch", Marion Lillie, we will search in vain for any reference to her in the Spott Kirk Session minutes for 1698, in spite of what is written in the Statistical Account. Here again Mr Martin has slipped up. There is no mention of witchcraft in the 1698 minutes, but the lengthy saga of Marion Lillie is exhaustively recorded in 1702 and 1703. It should be said also, that it is unlikely that Marion was "generally called" *the* rigwoody witch, for this is not a nickname, but a description. A rigwoody or rigwiddy witch is often taken to mean a wrinkled and ugly witch, but is more likely to have meant something akin to a "thoroughgoing" or "out-and-out" witch; one in danger of the "widdy" or rope. Burns mentions "rigwoody hags" in Tam o' Shanter, the Saltoun Kirk Session minutes record a woman being fined forty shillings in 1646 for calling another a "rigwoody witch", and as we shall see, the Spott records mention one James Baillie confronting Marion Lillie, and calling her *a* rigwoody witch.

At a meeting of Spott Kirk Session on 15th November 1702, the minister informed his elders that Robert Kemp, weaver in Spott, and his mother Marion Lillie had come to him complaining that Marion's good name had been slandered by Janet Logan. (We should remember that in Scotland in those days married women usually kept their own surnames, while their children inherited the surname of their father. Marion, therefore, had obviously been married to a man named Kemp, and was now presumably a widow.) The minister had decided to bring Marion and her son along, so that they could lay their complaint formally, and so that they could be questioned about the matter. The Session agreed to hear them, and they were called in.

Marion claimed that Janet Logan had spoken evil things about her to her son Robert Kemp. Kemp related how a few days previously he had been passing Janet Logan's door, and had heard her son William roaring and making a great noise. He went in to see what was going on, and Janet Logan greeted him with, "Heart hatred is slockened now!" Realising that Janet meant that someone was harming her son by witchcraft out of spite, Kemp asked whom she was blaming. Janet replied bluntly that she was blaming Kemp's mother, and affirmed that Marion had been doing the Devil's work against her and her family since August. This was said in the presence of others, who could confirm Kemp's claim. Marion added that the following day, Janet Logan had confronted her when she was alone in her own home, and threatened to tear her to pieces if her son died.

Marion requested that the Session should summon Janet Logan, require her to prove her accusations, and punish her accordingly if she failed to do so. It is often believed nowadays that in 17th Century Scotland all one had to do was point the finger at some poor innocent and call her "witch", and she would be immediately dragged off to the stake. Nothing could be further from the truth. The Kirk took slander very seriously, particularly if imputations of witchcraft were involved, and the kirk session minutes of East Lothian are full of cases where one parishioner calls another "witch", and an exhaustive investigation is set in motion, which almost always ends with the slanderer being forced to apologise to the injured party, often publicly before the congregation in the most humiliating circumstances. The Church of Scotland is not entirely blameless as far as witchcraft persecution is concerned, but if you called your neighbour a witch without good reason, you were running the severe risk of bringing down salutary punishment on your own head.

Having considered "the grossness of the scandal" Spott Kirk Session decided to summon Janet Logan to appear before them on the following Sunday along with the two witnesses who had heard Janet say to Robert Kemp that his mother was doing the Devil's work. Janet duly turned up, and admitted that she did indeed believe that Marion had been doing the Devil's work against her. She admitted threatening to tear her to pieces if her son died, and claimed that his health had improved since she confronted Marion. The Session dispensed with examining the witnesses, since Janet had admitted most of what was charged against her, and they postponed their decision until the next meeting.

On December 3rd, the Kirk Session decided that it would be helpful to question Janet Logan further about precisely why it was she felt that Marion Lillie was doing the Devil's work against her, and she was therefore summoned to appear three days later on December 6th to explain herself before the Session, in the presence of Marion and her son. On the appointed day, Janet stated that three years previously her son William had tried to get Robert Kemp to take him on as an apprentice, but Marion had abruptly turned him down on her son's behalf. On another occasion, Marion came into Janet's house looking for fire, and noticed William was reading a book. Marion asked, "Are you reading, Will?" and William replied, "Yes." Shortly after this apparently innocent exchange William fell ill, was struck blind and dumb, and was "not right" for a month after that.

The Kirk Session might well have thought that this was pretty thin evidence on which to base accusations of witchcraft, but Janet Logan went on to insist that Marion had been notorious as a witch for many years. Her own daughter-in-law had called her a witch to her face several years previously. Also, when William Colme had forbidden her to keep a tethered ewe, Marion threatened to make him repent it, and two of his mares subsequently ran mad and died. James Baillie had confronted Marion on the main road through Spott village, calling her a rigwoody witch and had "blooded her in the face". (This ritual was also known as "scoring above the breath". It was an antidote to witchcraft, and the belief was that drawing blood from the witch would undo the evil that she was trying to work on the victim.) Janet Logan then went on to describe how on the day she went to Marion's house, three adults were insufficient to hold her son down in his bed. She admitted that she had threatened to tear Marion to pieces, and said that no sooner had she reached home, than her son began to settle, and he had been improving ever since.

Robert Kemp then demanded that Janet should be required to prove her allegations, adding that he was sure she would be unable to do so. Having run out of time, the Kirk Session postponed further discussion until their next meeting.

On 13th December, having spoken privately to the minister beforehand, Janet Logan appeared with another catalogue of accusations against Marion Lillie. Some years before, Catherine Deans, who was living in Bowden, came back to Spott to see her friends and relatives. She was pregnant with her first child. At some point during this visit, Marion had gripped her belly, and shortly afterwards Catherine was seized by a pain which never abated till she gave birth to a stillborn child six weeks later. Janet Logan also claimed that Marion's son Robert Kemp had hanged a mad dog over her cow's fodder, and since then her cow was giving less milk than before. On another occasion, Marion had laid a pair of stockings in the road in front of Janet's door. They lay there all day until a passer-by threw them in at Janet's door, thinking they must be hers. Janet lifted them with a pair of tongs and replaced them on the road, and when night fell Marion came and took them away.

The Session now suspected that they were dealing with something more serious than a simple case of slander, and decided to seek advice from the Presbytery, the Kirk's next-highest administrative level. The Presbytery advised that Janet Logan would have to prove her accusations against Marion, and Marion herself insisted that Janet should be made to do so. Janet asserted that several people could testify to the truth of her claims, and requested that the Kirk Session should summon them and take their statements. Janet added that within the past few days, Marion had prayed that the heavy curse of God might fall upon her and anyone who spoke to her. The Session decided to call Janet's witnesses to their next meeting.

On 7th January 1703 Marion, Janet, and eight witnesses attended the Kirk Session meeting. Firstly, William Colme in Spott testified that he had been present in the "Barlae Court" (a local court for regulating grazings, boundaries etc.) about ten years previously, when Marion Lillie had been refused permission to keep a ewe tethered on the green. She had commented that some of them would rue it before the year was out. A few weeks later Colme had gone to Pressmennan Wood to buy timber, when he got a message to return home as his mare was dying. The mare ran mad and died in the evening, leaving a young foal. He borrowed a mare in milk from Robert Burnet, and managed to get her to feed the foal. Next morning Colme found her sitting on her rump like a dog, unable to move. He called in a horse doctor who told him that supposing he had five hundred merks to spend on the mare, he need not bother, as it would do no good. The horse doctor said that he suspected Colme was envied by someone, and that either seven or nine of his beasts would die before the business was at an end. Shortly afterwards, one of his hens came out of the barn with a number of chicks. Seven of them fell over, swelled up, and died. Colme finished by saying that Marion was held to be a witch by the people of the neighbourhood, and that he had heard Janet Logan say her son had expressed a wish to draw blood from her.

Jean Lochard in Spott stated that Catherine Deans had told her how Marion Lillie greeted her as she passed through Spott on horseback with her husband. Marion asked her how she was doing, laid her hand on her belly, then gripped it. Half a mile further on she was seized with pain, and as she seemed about to faint, her husband lifted her down from the horse. She continued to feel unwell until she gave birth to her first child, which died soon after. Jean also testified that that she had heard Marion Lillie bid the curse of God come down on Janet Logan and all who listened to her.

Margaret Wightman, a 56 year old widow, was present when Marion Lillie gripped Catherine Deans's belly, and confirmed that the young woman fell sick, that her husband had to lift her from their horse, and that she had felt the pain of Marion's grip until her child was born.

James Baillie, when asked if he had heard that Marion Lillie was supposed to be a witch, answered that this was the word going through the countryside, and that he had heard it even before he came to live in Spott.

John Guilly stated that he had heard the story in Spott about Janet Logan's son recovering after Janet had confronted Marion Lillie. Janet Grieve, a girl of 19, said that on the morning in question she had heard Janet Whyte ask Janet Logan's daughter how her brother Will was, and heard her say he was no better. She went in to see him in the evening and saw him looking better, and speaking quite sensibly. Barbara Caulder denied that she had ever called Marion Lillie a witch, but Jane Muet said that she had heard people say that Janet Logan's son grew better after his mother had gone in to Marion Lillie. John Whyte testified that Janet's son was ill in the morning and better at night, and Janet Whyte, a girl of 18, stated that when she went out with the cow that day in the morning, she asked Janet Logan's daughter Elizabeth how her brother was, and was told he was no better. When she came back from the fair in the evening she went in to see him, and saw an improvement. He had been better ever since.

Almost all of the witnesses testified that it was the common belief that Marion Lillie was a witch.

At their next meeting, after much discussion, Spott Kirk Session decided that Janet Logan had in fact proved several of her accusations against Marion Lillie. Taking the seriousness of the case into consideration, the Session resolved to seek the opinion of the Presbytery once again. Was Janet Logan to be censured as a slanderer, now that she had proved her charges against Marion Lillie? And what was the Session to do next about Marion? On 31st January the minister announced the decision of the Presbytery to the Kirk Session. Janet was not to be held guilty of slander, Marion was to be publicly rebuked before the congregation for her cursing and bitter imprecations against Janet, and Marion should be referred to the civil magistrate "for further tryall in these matters".

Marion was called in again on 14th February and questioned about her knowledge of witchcraft and whether she had ever made a compact with the Devil. She was urged to confess, but instead she emphatically denied knowing anything about such matters. The minister then informed her that she was to be publicly rebuked before the congregation for calling down curses on Janet Logan.

Before that happened, however, it next came to light that another woman in Spott parish, Janet Haliburton, had suffered at Marion's hands in the same way as Catherine Deans. When she was visited by the minister Janet told him that a year previously, when she was pregnant, Marion Lillie came into her house while she was baking. Janet invited her to sit down and gave her a piece of bread. Marion reached over, laid her hand on Janet's belly, gripped it, and said, "What, woman? Are you not growing big yet?" Two or three days later Janet miscarried. She said she could think of nothing else that might have brought on the miscarriage, but she would not go so far as to say that Marion's touching her was the cause. It was decided that the minister and two of the elders should go and speak to Marion yet again. When they did so, Marion said that she had meant no harm by laying her hand on Janet Haliburton's belly. Tackled again about cursing Janet Logan, she not only showed no regret but rather tried to vindicate herself.

On April 4th the minister announced that Marion had moderated her attitude, and that she now acknowledged her sin in cursing Janet Logan. The Session thus decided that it was time for her to make her public repentance, which she duly carried out the following Sunday.

Finally, on April 18th, five months after the saga had begun, the minister reported to the Kirk Session the fact that Marion had done public penance as required, and that the church had proceeded as far as it could as regards witchcraft. Any further investigation was to be left to the civil magistrate.

The Kirk Session of Spott had done all that the law allowed it to do. Church courts were empowered to question suspects about witchcraft, but were not qualified to put witchcraft suspects on trial. The civil magistrate could arrange for imprisonment and further interrogation, and if sufficient evidence, or a confession, was obtained, the suspect could be sent for trial at the High Court, or a commission could be sought from the Privy Council for a local trial.

In Marion's case the civil magistrate would presumably be the Laird of Spott or his baron baillies. Incidentally, when the Presbytery recommended that Marion should be handed over to the civil magistrate "for further tryall", we are not talking about a "trial" in the modern sense of the word. In the idiom of the 17th and early 18th Centuries, "trying" a suspect meant questioning her, and "trial" meant interrogation. What we would now call a trial was then usually termed an "assize". Whether the civil magistrate ever bestirred himself to question Marion, we do not know, but Marion's reputation and the hearsay evidence which convinced the minister and elders of Spott is unlikely to have convinced a court of law in early 18th Century Scotland. There is no record of Marion ever standing trial, either in the records of the High Court, or in the records of the Privy Council. Since these were the only bodies entitled to try her, it is probably safe to say that no such trial ever took place.

There may be those, determined to uphold Scotland's reputation for cruel and merciless witch persecution, who will prefer to believe the "tradition" so dear to local historians that Marion Lillie was indeed burned at the Witches' Stone, in spite of the lack of any shred of evidence for such a turn of events. Unfortunately for "tradition", the Spott burial register records quite plainly in 1705, "Febry 11th. Deceased Marion Lillie in Spott & was interred at this kirk", and the record of parish expenses for the period 30th January to 23rd April 1705 records, "To bell and mortcloth to Marion Lillie 02-10-00."

No convicted and executed witch would have been buried in the consecrated ground of a parish churchyard, and indeed no executed witch *could* have been buried there, since the requisite sentence explicitly stated that the condemned witch should be strangled at a stake *and her body burnt to ashes*. There can be no doubt that in spite of her reputation, Marion died a natural death in April 1705, and was buried in Spott kirkyard with the usual ceremonial trappings of bell and mortcloth.

Thus, whoever was put to death at the Witches' Stone, it was not the much maligned Marion Lillie, who, far from being burned at the stake, was never even put on trial.

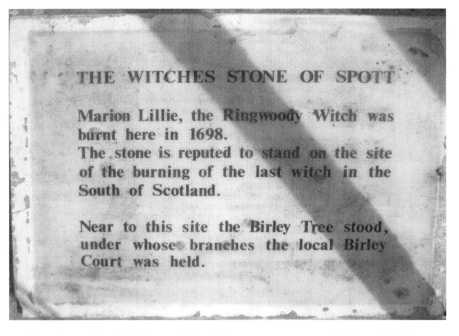

THE WITCHES STONE OF SPOTT

Marion Lillie, the Ringwoody Witch was burnt here in 1698.
The stone is reputed to stand on the site of the burning of the last witch in the South of Scotland.

Near to this site the Birley Tree stood, under whose branches the local Birley Court was held.

The plaque beside the Witches' Stone says wrongly that Marion Lillie was burnt here. In fact Marion never stood trial for witchcraft, and died a natural death in 1705.

Bibliography

Primary Sources:

National Archives of Scotland :
Kirk Session Minutes, filed under CH2.
Presbytery Minutes, also CH2.
Haddington Burgh Records, filed under GD1/413.
Justiciary Court Records, including boxes of "Court Processes"
(JC26), High Court Minute Books (JC6), and the Books of
Adjournal (JC2).
The Register of the Privy Council, ed. John Hill Burton,
Edinburgh, 1877.

Secondary Sources:

Larner, C., Hyde, C. McLachlan, Hugh V. *A Source-book of Scottish
witchcraft*. Glasgow, 1977, reprinted The Grimsay Press, 2005.

Normand, l. and Roberts, G. *Witchcraft in Early Modern Scotland*,
Exeter, 2000.
Deals very fully with The North Berwick witches.

Robertson, David M. *Goodnight My Servants All*. Glasgow, The
Grimsay Press, 2008.
*A full collection of references to witchcraft in East Lothian from
court and church records "translated" into modern English. It will
enable the interested reader to trace the original sources of the
cases presented in "Wise wives and warlocks".*

Index

Lightning Source UK Ltd.
Milton Keynes UK
UKOW04f1346250615

254117UK00002B/61/P